Contents

AF719489

About the author

Jordan Smith is an engineer, an investor and a man filled with a zest for achieving financial freedom as early as life may allow. He has a Bachelor's Degree in Mechanical and Aeronautical Engineering from the University of Pretoria where he graduated with distinction. He continued his academic development across a wide range of fields such as Strategic Management at the Duke University as well as Management Accounting with the Charted Institute of Management Accountants (CIMA).

His academic accolades have been a strength and driving force during his relentless pursuit to discover how one would realise financial freedom as young as possible. In pursuit of this understanding, he has applied his logical and critical thinking mind to the challenge. Through investing in a broad spectrum of financial assets and identifying which of those have proven to generate the best yield, he has gained significant insight into the workings of the personal financial world.

Although, as an engineer, he has grown at a significant rate in his career in the corporate world, he has also ensured that he methodically continued to nurture his personal investment portfolio, growing assets that produce passive income.

Aside from being passionate about his own financial future he places a strong focus during his spare time towards sharing knowledge through pro bono consultations, financial talks as well as presentations in low-income areas. Thus, providing guidance where he can on some of the basic life principles followed by the wealthy.

In essence, he is a man driven by his belief that in this world there is space for all to be financially free.

Forword

I often lay awake at night envisioning myself changing the world, exploring ideas that I could bring into reality. Ultimately, this book is a means to that end. Walking through everyday life I encounter far too few people who are financially secure, who feel rich and who don't lay awake stressed over how to support their families.

Before my wife and I close our eyes each evening we share a moment of gratitude for the blessings we have received. That time spent saying thank you for all we have has had a profound impact on the vision of how I will change the world.

Through this book, or more accurately, this memoir and thought journal, I hope to provide financial insights to those I walk past each day so that the number of faces lined with worry reduces, if even only by a thousandth of a percent.

So please feel free to indulge yourself in critically analysing the pages that follow which discuss the successes and failures of my life thus far.

Introduction

A sophist may ask, "Is being employed in a well-paid, stable profession truly what is best for one's life?"

It is a common dream to have financial freedom, to not live month to month, pay cheque to pay cheque. Why then, do most of us find ourselves making others richer, whilst leaving ourselves barely able to pay our bills? We go to work each day, expending our energy only to help the rich earn more. When we get home, we have nothing left to give, no energy left to change our trajectory. Nothing left to reach financial freedom.

This point was quite a challenging realisation to internalise for me, grasping the fact that, climbing the ladder of our society's classic idea of success was not necessarily the path to financial freedom. We all grow up being taught that career success equates to financial success. Sadly, often more than not, following that principle has led many people, who were highly successful in their careers, to a point where their retirement funds have run out and they are required to lean on their family to support them in their old age.

When did we fall into this trap? I'm an engineer by trade, which is why I like to understand how different moving parts create a certain outcome. From my assessment, this phenomenon has always been and always will be. An employee can be all to likened to a slave during the Egyptian or Roman times or to a peasant during the Feudal times. Like a slave or peasant an employee expends their life's energy working to enrich their master, lord or employer.

Now before we begin to see the world through the eyes of Karl Marx and feel locked into depression and despair, there is one pertinent difference between being an employee of today compared to that of the enricher of others from the past, and that is the freedom of choice. Today we are blessed with the freedom to choose whether we want to work towards somebody else's riches, or whether we would prefer to generate our own. Unlike in Marx's assessment, the reality is that in today's world, an amalgamation of capitalism and socialism, we maintain our freedom of choice. The freedom to choose our own path to financial freedom.

So, this begs the question, "Should I choose to quit my job, and venture out on my own, taking on the risks of entrepreneurship, or should I continue along the line of the worker, also known as stable employment?"

I say, why not do both. While yes, there certainly are weaknesses when it comes to employment, however it would be pertinent to consider the strengths as well. Personally, I would advise against acting to hastily to cut the bonds of employment. Rather, I would advise that one utilises the power of leveraging guaranteed income to make oneself rich. After all, if you are making somebody else rich while working 9 to 5, often longer, why not make a little for yourself, or better yet, why not make more than a little for yourself.

Now, how does one go about leveraging guaranteed income?

How does one actually get rich?

The pages that follow details some of the key concepts and insights into doing just that. The aim of this book is to act as a guide on some of the core principles that will assist with making the move from working for money to making money.

Chapter 1:

In the beginning

The grandeur of youthful thinking

The year was 2003, my friend Ryan and I, were in his room listening to the latest Now CD, dreaming about how we were going to change the world. At the age of nine no dream was too big; the world was filled with endless possibilities and life seemed infinite.

While scrolling through songs on his desk top computer we finally come up with our grand idea, our secret trick to achieving ultimate greatness.

Unable to contain our exhilaration nor keep the secret to ourselves we ran through to the lounge, almost tripping over Ryans ever playful Labrador, we burst into the room and with childish excitement interrupted our mother's conversation, as young children often do. Battling for breath, elated with enthusiasm we both began talking over one another. Finally, while our mothers waited patiently with smiles of endearment, we managed to string together a few coherent words, taking our caring spectators through the secret plan.

“Mom, Auntie Margret, we know what we going to be when we grow up.” I panted. “We’re going to be doctors AND engineers.” Ryan exclaimed. “We’ll build during the week…”, “and work as doctors on the weekend when the building for the week finishes.” Ryan and I exhaled in unison.

I can remember the adoration in our mothers’ eyes and being nine our excitement was only amplified by the loving and proud laugh that escaped from the unsuspecting audience we had chosen to pitch our idea to.

Ten years later Ryan and I had enrolled in Medicine and Engineering respectively. Several years after that Ryan and I had both graduated, ready to begin the journey of success we had conjured up in our dreams all those years ago.

It is a common aspiration of parents to dream of their child becoming a doctor or an engineer, understandably so. Society has great respect for both fields and often more than not these professions are afforded high paying salaries. Most importantly they provide the ultimate assurance any parent could want for their child, income security.

But there is a core principle which this dream neglects to consider which makes it ultimately flawed and that is that in life, there are three types of people. I call them workers, earners and makers. Furthermore, it is common for highly qualified individuals, such as doctors or engineers, to find themselves on the opposite side of the financially free.

Workers, Earners and Makers

I can clearly recall the day that I came to realise the fact that in life there are workers, earners and makers and that not all doctors nor engineers are guaranteed financial success. What etched this memory in my mind was the shocking realisation of who made up the category of workers.

I recall standing beside the fire on a hot summer evening, a bit of perspiration on my brow and a cold beverage in hand, I was enthralled in a conversation with a group of doctors who were busy specialising in a variety of fields. After a while the topic moved over to finance where stresses around money and living expenses were being shared. To my astonishment this group of highly successful doctors were experiencing severe financial stress. The next day, I could not shake the feeling of disbelief and so I began to contemplate how it could be possible that high earning individuals were coming short on funds each month. Over the years I have begun to understand precisely what drives the common story of large salary earning individuals feeling high amounts of financial pressure.

It all comes down to a simple core principle. There are typically three types of people in the modern financial system, namely workers, earners, and makers. Each has a very distinctive set of characteristics. In order to understand how it is possible for a doctor, engineer or any other high paying discipline to be under financial strain despite their high paying salary it is best to grasp this core principle.

Workers: Money is a representation of value, that value in its simplest form is a measurement of effort. When an individual gives of their time or effort they generate money or value. A worker is an individual who works and expends effort for someone, a business, or an organisation in order to be compensated for that effort in the form of money. The amount of money they can earn is limited by the amount of effort they can expend. A worker is not necessarily an unskilled person. In fact, by definition, doctors can be considered workers because they earn by the hour. Strictly speaking, most service rendering industries would fall within this category. The other key trait generally associated with the worker category is that the individuals who render services or expend effort in order to be paid often are specialised in that one field and do not have a strong understanding or skill set in any other field.

This trend is highly prevalent in the medical field as doctors are required to store and know such high volumes of medical knowledge that they do not have the time nor capacity to expand their expertise into other fields. Which is why a considerable number of doctors can struggle financially. Added to this, comes the stress that once a worker stops working, so does the value they generate cease to be created and thus their income stream disappears.

Earners: Usually considered the Jack of all trades type of individual, this category is generally a leader of people and usually a leader of workers, however the earner still earns for a company or organisation. Earners typically have a fair understanding of finances and profit generation though typically do not have the vision of an entrepreneur. Thus, they find themselves earning for others, assisting the workers generate value through their effort and ensuring that more value roles in than what roles out. With their understanding of finance, earners often retire comfortably having managed to save up and invest effectively to live off their retirement until they leave the remainder of their estate to their children.

Makers: The last category is that of the maker, someone who is creative and able to see where value can be generated through a new idea or through a new approach. Sometimes a maker is even someone who identifies a strong business model and replicates it. Makers are the entrepreneurs of our world, the people who employ others, the ones who provide a platform for earners to guide their work force.

My good friend from primary school comes to mind, he wasn't the strongest at academics and chose rather than to go to university, he would earn his trade in plumbing. He started off as a plumber for a plumbing business, gaining experience and improving his skills, but most importantly, he learned how a plumbing business operated. Within three years he had branched off from his original employment and struck out on his own. Two years later he had three plumbers and one apprentice working for him. Now, he has several managers who are the earners, guiding his work force of plumbers all generating value through their effort.

I have often wondered what leads people to each category, is it natural ability, personal life circumstance or a matter of choice? I have concluded that without a doubt, it is a matter of choice. To choose whether one wants to be a worker, an earner or a maker. Let's look further then at what factors one should consider when choosing and how one makes that choice.

Employment versus Entrepreneurship

A renowned author, named Robert Kiyosaki, author of *Rich Dad Poor Dad,* is known to express a rather similar view about the world. Kiyosaki is a strong advocate for working towards securing passive income rather than a secure well-paying job or in other words working towards becoming a maker rather than staying a worker.

Side Comment: Passive income, put simply, is money that is received with minimal to no effort from oneself.

Kiyosaki is not the only famous author or successful entrepreneur to encourage becoming your own boss and better yet to become an employer of employees. The natural question then is, which is the correct path? That of working towards being one of the wealthy success stories or that of the stable safe income of employment. All things being equal, it comes down to one main factor, the risk of income security. Choosing between the two paths, requires self-assessment. One must decide what is more important, the security in knowing that your pay cheque is guaranteed or whether the possibility of higher earnings is better suited to your aspirations. The age old saying comes to mind, "High risk, high reward."

Let's pause for a moment, surely one doesn't have to choose between the two, why can't one follow both paths? If you are anything like me, you would find yourself asking exactly that. Thus far in my financial journey I have followed precisely that philosophy. Having a stable income, while being a worker and later on an earner, has enabled me to leverage the power of another entity's capital to generate a positive passive income cash flow for myself, essentially making money for nothing other than the fact that my stable salary is a "guarantee" against a loan.

My guaranteed income has given banks and other lending parties the confidence that I will be able to meet monthly payments and thus they have been willing to loan me money. Using this money, I have purchased positive passive income generating assets which have added to my overall monthly income as well as wealth. To put it simply, the power of good debt is something that has been one of, if not the biggest contributing factors, to my financial success thus far.

The power of leveraging your guaranteed income to generate more money off someone else's money may sound too good to be true. In reality, it can be a solution to generating one's fortune. It all comes down to understanding the financial affordability of your employment income and ensuring that you do not over-stretch your debts payable. Maintaining your debt-to-income ratio in a healthy state is critical to ensuring that the magical solution of income leveraging remains just that and doesn't transform into a state of bad debt. More on this in Chapter 2.

Above the financial implications of deciding between the path of employment and entrepreneurship, i.e. the choice of being a worker, earner or maker, is the factor of time. Commonly it is found that the path of employment provides the luxury of being able to "knock off" when going home without the need to worry about the future of the company, whereas self-employment or entrepreneurship does not afford that indulgence. When running your own business there is no 9 to 5, but rather this path calls for 24/7 dedication. Saying that though, being your own boss allows for one to decide when and where to work. I think of family friends of mine who are entrepreneurs that seem to be perpetually on vacation. They truly are financially free having achieved vast sums of passive income.

There are a few other factors to reflect on when deciding on which path to follow on your financial journey, however, the points above, in my opinion, are the most pertinent to consider. My personal plan is to take the approach of following both paths. Initially, I started off fully focused on the path of employment, developing my guaranteed income. Gradually, I have begun shifting my focus and energy over to the path of entrepreneurship, employing the power of income leveraging, increasing my debt-to-income ratio, being cautious not to overextend, with the ultimate goal of shifting completely to the path of being a maker and an entrepreneur (i.e. generating passive income). In Chapter 2 we will discuss the possible paths to financial freedom shedding further light on the possibility of retiring early.

Thoughts on Early Retirement

Before considering how to achieve early retirement, let us discuss the secret of the rich. Firstly, the "secret" of the rich is not a particularly close guarded one, but, rather an unfortunate consequence of the educational system most of the world employs. Note I use the word "employs" purposefully, as our educational system is designed to generate employees/workers rather than entrepreneurs. It is geared towards creating the work force which keeps our economic wheel turning. The topic of the modern world's educational system is subject to extensive debate, but we will not focus on what should be taught and why, rather, we will explore what it is that isn't taught.

The secret can be summarised into two words, positive cashflow. Cash flowing in rather than out. This can sound like an oversimplification. Well, I can honestly say that it isn't, acquiring positive cashflow assets is simple. The difficulty is understanding and achieving or acquiring efficient high return, high cash flow assets that are efficient in their time and energy input requirements.

Let's delve further and investigate various types of potential financial assets and compare their virtues, risks and implications. The following summary table illustrates only a few of the important aspects of common financial assets available in the modern world and is by no means a comprehensive list.

Side Comment: The figures contained in Table 1 are subject to the ever-changing market and are listed as indicative values in order to provide understanding of the various asset classes, their virtues and risks. The asset descriptions have also been written in an overly simplified manner again as a means to provide understanding.

Later, we will discuss the various methods of acquiring each type of asset, thus equipping you with the necessary tools and knowledge to start working towards financial freedom. After studying the table, and before we get to the details of working towards financial freedom, it would be best to define what it would mean and look like for each individual, after all what one person might classify as a picture of financial freedom differs from the next. In the next chapter we will go through the three classic ideas of financial freedom and the respective paths to follow in order to achieve them.

Asset Class	Description of asset	Risks
	Property Rentals	
Short term rentals	Primarily holiday letting	Vacancies Rental defaulting
Long term rentals	Typical housing rentals - rooms, apartments & houses	Vacancies Rental defaulting
Commercial rentals	Rental of property to a retail or office space business	Vacancies Rental defaulting
Industrial rentals	Rental of property to a production or operation facilities	Vacancies Rental defaulting
	Shares & Stocks	
Stocks/Shares	Shares of a business purchased through the stock market – often yielding dividends	Exposed to market turbulence
Business ownership	Earnings from profit payout	High risk of failure/bankruptcy
	Interest	
High-Yield savings bank account interest	Federally insured savings account aiming to yield high interest	Low risk
Certificates of Deposit	Longer term saving commitments 3 months to 5 years or more	Low risk
Money market accounts	Similar to online high-yield savings bank accounts	Low risk
	Bonds	
Bond Mutual Funds	Essentially a loan to a government or corporation.	Low risk
Bond ETFs	A combined set of bonds	Low risk
	Unit Trusts	
Income Funds	A mix of investments typically in cash and bonds managed by a financial institution	High management fees
Aggressive Funds	A mix of assets typically in shares and/or offshore investments managed by a financial institution	High management fees & exposed to market turbulence

Table 1: Financial Assets Summary

Benefits	Typical yield above inflation p.a.	Passive income, Interest or Capital gains
Property Rentals		
Little effort required for high returns Control over asset	1 – infinite (avg. 10%)	Passive & Capital Gains
Lower risk of vacancies Low effort required to acquire income Control over asset	1 – infinite (avg. 10%)	Passive & Capital Gains
Low effort required for high returns Control over asset	1 – infinite (avg. 10%)	Passive & Capital Gains
Little effort required for high returns Control over asset	1 – infinite (avg. 10%)	Passive & Capital Gains
Shares & Stocks		
No effort required	0 - 10%	Passive & Capital Gains
Control over asset Typically yields high returns	1 - infinite	Passive
Interest		
No effort required	1%	Capital Gains
No effort required	2%	Capital Gains
No effort required	1%	Capital Gains
Bonds		
No effort required	3%	Interest
No effort required	3%	Interest
Unit Trusts		
No effort required	1-3%	Capital Gains
No effort required	7% or more	Capital Gains

Table 1 continued: Financial Assets Summary

Chapter 2:

What are the paths to financial freedom?

Three diverging paths

Knowing that each person has their own dreams and aspirations is a commonly understood concept. A lesser-known concept, but still widely accepted, is that the definition of financial success differs from person to person. One person may view being able to settle down on a small plot of land with their family as true financial success, another may feel that cruising around the world on a super yacht is the true measure of having reached financial freedom. Whichever way one may envision the measurement of financial freedom, a common aspect is often left out of that vision. Which leads me to a little-known concept, there are different paths to achieving financial success.

Fundamentally, there are typically three financial means of being able to afford the luxuries conjured up in people's lifelong dreams and aspirations regardless of which ever romantic image of success an individual may visualise.

The first, most understood and followed model of achieving financial freedom, is that of a retirement fund. The approach of taking a set portion of one's earnings each month, or payment period, and investing into various interest bearing or capital gains driven assets. Typical asset examples are Bonds, Unit Trusts, Investment Funds and Interest Yielding Banking Facilities.

Another commonly known model, the second model, involves entrepreneurship, where a business is developed and grown during one's lifetime to a point where it is self-sustaining and requires little to no input, while yielding profit payouts that pay for ones living expenses.

The third, lesser-known model is an amalgamation of both the first and second models. It is based on a concept introduced in Chapter 1, the power of income leveraging. This model involves leveraging one's income to acquire positive cash flow passive income assets using loans or in other words *other people's money* (OPM) which is gradually paid back during ones working career using the income that the assets generate. The income producing assets are then free to fund ones living expenses thus enabling financial freedom. Often more than not, these assets return more than what is necessary to pay the monthly loan amount providing additional income. This additional income is then combined with the savings originating from one's monthly earnings and is invested by the same means as discussed in first model or into high-risk investments on the stock market.

Deciding which model to follow is dependent on personal preference. Let's explore each one a little deeper. We will investigate their workings, benefits as well as risks so that an informed decision can be made on which model's path one should choose to follow.

Model 1: Old school retirement plan

The method of putting away a portion of one's earnings each month into a retirement fund is something that seems to have been around since the dawn of time. In reality, when viewed from a historical perspective retirement plans as viewed today are actually a fairly modern invention. The earliest form of retirement plans looked vastly different compared to its modern counterpart, often associated with a cacophony of words of advice from all sorts of investment advisors.

The first concept of a pension fund was established during the times of the Roman empire, where those who had served in the military were provided with a state pension. Interestingly, the fall of the once great empire is inextricably linked to defaulting on payment of that state provided pensions. (Robert L. Clark, 2003) The next significant development in the history of retirement and pension funds was when, in the 19th century, the German Chancellor, Otto Von Bismarck, announced that forced retirement would be applicable to anyone over the age of 70 years old, he further announced that he would pay those people a pension. (Weisman, 1999) The idea began to catch on and by the 1920s, not only were governments providing pensions to state workers, but a variety of industries in America were offering pensions as well. (Laskow, 2014)

From there retirement planning has joined the globalisation trend, where it has transformed into the modern version of today.

The modern worlds retirement financial planning has evolved from an employer simply paying out a periodical payout, often monthly, to one where a multitude of investments are made during one's lifetime into several financial assets, complicating the matter to a point where the general person simply hands over their financial planning to a financial planner. The transformation into the complex multi-fund concoction investment portfolios found today began when companies decided to no longer provide a guaranteed pension payment until the retiree's death but rather company's would provide a means of assisting an individual make monthly payments into an investment fund, typically referred to as a pension or provident fund. It is not uncommon for these funds to underperform inflation over the period of a person's lifetime.

So, knowing that and to compensate for it most people have had to make the choice, to reduce their living standards upon retirement, known as "downsizing when retiring", or to become savvy saving individuals increasing their portion of savings put towards retirement. Unfortunately, the daunting task of choosing which assets to invest in inevitably comes up and generally that is when people seek out a financial advisor. Sadly, the financial advisors all to often recommend their clients to diversify their investments. Whenever I hear the words "diversification of investments", I hear reduction of risk and where there is risk reduction there is a reduction in the return on investment. It is no surprise then, that following this methodology has left many people living with their children and or grandchildren because their retirement funds ran out.

Now, to be clear, I am not saying that this methodology is without its merits and by no means am I implying that seeking out guidance from a professional financial advisor is a bad decision. I am simply pointing out the risks involved in choosing this path so that an informed decision can be made when walking down the classic retirement lane. Which leads me to my next point, there is without a doubt at least one pro to leisurely walking this lane, it requires little to no effort. One's focus can be based solely on their career which may enable a person to excel further in their career than if they were to have chosen another path, which in turn can lead to a higher paycheck, a higher amount being saved each month and ultimately a larger retirement fund.

Model 2: High risk plan for achieving financial freedom

Choosing the path of starting a business to fund one's retirement is not for the faint hearted. Most startup businesses fail in their first few years leaving the founder feeling disappointed. It is those that stick at it and persevere that end up making a success of walking the path of entrepreneurship.

I am fortunate enough to have worked with and for some highly successful entrepreneurs. I have also had the opportunity to grow up personally knowing other successful entrepreneurs.

I won't be going into how they made a success of their businesses as each person's story differs, however they all did have one common trait, they all have endless quantities of perseverance. So, rather than discussing the secrets to start a business as there are countless, let's unravel what it is that each business has in common allowing the respective founder and/or owner to be on perpetual vacation. Their, they all had one common attribute in their enterprises. In each of their business they had set up a reliable team who were more than capable of running the operations without their involvement. These individuals would join a board meeting occasionally to assess the state of the business or they might visit one of the operations sites to see how each employee was getting along.

Achieving this kind of financial freedom, I am sure sounds like every person's dream, though let us not forget that these individuals built these businesses passing through immense hurdles to achieve the end results and all are astute business minded people. Now, one shouldn't lose hope because having such a set of accolades as described above seems unachievable, rather one could consider the middle ground, or otherwise known as, the best of both worlds. So, let's see how one can have their cake and eat it too.

Model 3: Best of both worlds'

So far in my financial journey, I can truly attest to the possibilities and power of combining both investing for long term capital gains or interest and the power of income leveraging enabling the use of OPM.

Ok, so earlier we established the principal of using our income to gain access to OPM, but how and why would people simply give us money? The answer lies in the fact that the vast majority of people today invest according to model 1. If they are to invest this way, they would require some form of investment to put their money towards.

Let's explore an example, a person invests R 100 000.00 into a certificate deposit seeking 6.5% for a 5-year period. The bank has now gotten a capital sum of R 100 000.00 and committed to pay the investor a return of 6.5% p.a. on their capital amount. Well, how would the bank pay the investor? Banks don't produce any goods so sell, so how would they make the money? They simply loan that R 100 000.00 to someone else, they even loan it at a higher interest rate than what they promised the investor. That is how banks make their money. Now, taking the example further, let's say we have found a property we would like to purchase for R 100 000.00 with plans to rent it out, would it not be in the banks best interest to loan us that R 100 000.00, say at interest rate of 10% p.a. over 5 years? Of course, they would, but only if they knew we could pay the monthly instalments and that's where the income leveraging comes in, using the promise of our monthly income from our employer we can convince the bank that we are a safe bet. All that is left to complete the picture is for us to find a tenant willing to pay a monthly rental that would cover our monthly instalment. Thus, freeing us to leverage our monthly income once again.

To take this a step further, what if in the example above the monthly rental exceeded the required monthly payments? Well then, we would have achieved a positive cash flow and would have acquired a passive income asset. The final step is to then take all the extra money that other people are giving you and invest it into another asset, my preference during my youth has been to invest those funds into high-risk stock market assets, ones where I have had integrate knowledge about the share being purchased thus mitigating the risk. More on this topic in Chapter 5.

With the understanding of the three possible paths one can walk down it is possible to make an educated choice. My personal preference is to follow the third model, it makes the most sense to me and I quite like the idea of making money from other people's money. It is also quite clearly apparent that following the third path provides the opportunity to retire early especially when one considers that once a positive cash flow passive income asset is acquired it can be held indefinitely thus providing an endless stream of income.

However, before we delve into the details of making money from OPM, first, we must establish how to generate the initial means to get started.

Chapter 3:

Generating initial capital (budget management)

The value of money

To claim that I have achieved my success thus far in life due to pure genius would be a lie. In truth I owe most of, if not all, of my financial success to an ever-determined man, who I am fortunate enough to call dad.

Throughout my life he has encouraged me to push myself academically and most importantly he provided me with an education in financial management, teaching me life lessons that have been pivotal to my journey towards financial freedom.

I recall it was a typical hot summers day on the South Coast of South Africa when my father taught me one of my first financials lessons. My family and I strolled off the street and out of the sun into a small store off the beach front, blissfully embracing the cool air-conditioned breeze that blew down our backs as we walked through the store's doorway. My mother and father were perusing through the shop when I eyed a jar of Chappies bubble-gum, one Chappie was two cents at the time, I reached up almost knocking over the jar trying to grab one out and ran excitedly to my mother asking if she would buy it for me. Overhearing my request, my father came over and knelt down holding out his hand, "My boy, this Chappie is only something that you want, not something that you need. Today you will learn the value of money."

Harsh words one might think for a five-year-old child, however those words have stuck with me ever since. Now I am not saying I didn't throw a temper tantrum at the time; I am only human after all, but the principle of that idea has never left me and the lesson struck home. Internalising those words of wisdom my father shared with me that day, has helped me learn one of the most, if not the most important lesson in achieving financial freedom, do not spend above your means or in other words, put away money into savings. Or as George Clason puts it in his book *The Richest Man In Babylon*, "Pay yourself first."

This in truth is an oversimplification of the most important lessons in achieving financial freedom, as it is not helpful for one's money to stagnate in a savings account, thus not earning more money off the money saved, but more on this later, first we must look into the how's, why's, do's and don'ts of budgeting.

Budgeting 101

The following four easy steps will help establish a clear, simple and powerful tool to plan a practical and useful budget.

Step 1: Be realistic about and understand how much cash will flow into your "pocket" for the budgeting period (a typical budgeting period is a month, and I will utilise the two words synonymously) and write it down. The act of writing or typing the actual number is fundamental to psychologically recognising the number/value. I personally write the number down every month when I sit down for planning my budget regardless of whether or not it changed. Now, the cash flow into your account that one should budget according to, needs to meet the following two important criteria.

Firstly, it cannot be subject to maybes, or put in other words, the money needs to be guaranteed. For example, a salary is guaranteed, an agreed wage with an agreed number of hours that will be worked is guaranteed or a planned dividends payout that is being processed for clearance is guaranteed etc. Some examples of money that would not meet this criterion is money from overtime not yet worked, expected interest on an investment that has yet to materialise or be withdrawn, sales not yet achieved or dividends from profits not yet finalised etc.

Secondly, it must be liquid. What does cash being liquid mean? Money or cash that is liquid is money that can be paid over for the purchase of something without a time delay. Examples of liquid cash is coins and bank notes, money in a current account, money in an immediately accessible savings account etc.

Money that should not be used for budgeting would be savings in the stock market with time requirements for sale of those stocks, money saved in a long-term savings account (example Certificates of Deposit).

Understanding what cash will be available to budget on becomes more complex and difficult to understand as one's assets begin generating a positive cash flow and expenses begin being paid from money coming in from investments rather than from one's salary. That is why step 1 is crucial to budgeting effectively.

Step 2: Establish how much one plans on saving each month. Many sources of literature point to saving 10% of one's budgeted earnings each month. The quantity of savings really depends on the rate at which one chooses to become financially stable. Once decided, put the money away into a savings of some sort.

Side comment: Note how step 2 is not the payment of one's bills but rather it is payment into savings.

The act of consciously deciding on the quantity to be saved is a powerful tool for generating wealth and ultimately financial freedom. Deciding on the quantity to be saved, generates a natural motivation deep within, one that enables the mind to step up into the next gear working on solutions on how to achieve that goal. The act of solving financial problems is a key part of unlocking financial freedom and the only way to increase one's skill in this area is by tackling the challenge head on.

Step 3: List all of the bills to be paid during the period and write down the value in a column next to them. Again, the power of writing it down and "putting ink to paper" cannot be emphasised enough. Writing all of one's expenses in a list helps not only visualise ones living costs but also critically think about the necessity of each cost. Another added benefit of writing down all of ones living expenses is that it becomes less likely for an expense to go amiss in one's budget planning.

Step 4: Problem solve. I have found it inevitable that the expenses each month out way the income. Most people would then instinctively balance their expenses to their income by reducing their savings percentage. Usually I hear terms like, "I guess I just need to be more realistic about how much I can save each month." I strongly disagree with this pattern of thought.

Side comment: I purposefully phrased step 4 as "Problem solve" and not balance the budget. Remember our purpose here, it is not to make ends meet but to plan and enable financial freedom. Challenging oneself to come up with solutions to financial problems is fundamental to creating wealth.

But how can I solve the problem of not having enough money? The problem isn't that one doesn't have enough money, but rather that one hasn't come up with enough solutions, yet. So, what are these supposed solutions then? The simplest solution is to reduce ones living expenses. While this technically can be effective, it certainly doesn't bode well for living a luxurious lifestyle. My preference is to rather problem solve the income side of the budget challenge. To get the mind thinking, below I have listed some of the solutions I have implemented and later we will also go through some of them in further detail.

- Investment into short-term letting property.
- Investment into long-term rental property.
- Providing engineering solutions using my experience and knowledge
- Investing in dividend yielding stocks
- Providing financial planning services
- Starting small side business (Retail)

The solutions listed are only but a few ways in which one can solve their exceedance of expenses compared to their income. The most important aspect to note however is that the above list can be categorized into two groups, ones that required time as well as effort and ones that were passive income generators. I primarily focus on growing my passive income and would advise doing the same to achieve financial freedom. The following table visually summarises the fundamental budgeting principles discussed thus far.

	Income (P+MA)	
	Description	**Amount**
	Salary	R15 000
	Rental Income (Flat 1)	3500
Step 1: Understand your income	Services Rendered Income	1400
	Stock Dividends	100
	Total Income	**R20 000**
	Savings and Expenses (P+MA)	
Step 2: Pay yourself first	**Description**	**Amount**
	Savings (Pay yourself first)	R 2 000.00
	Mortgage	R 5 000.00
	Housing rates, water and taxes	R 1 200.00
	Rental flat 1 bond repayment	R 2 000.00
	Rental flat 1 rates & taxes	R 500.00
Step 3: List your expenses	Rental flat 1 levees	R 500.00
	Gym	R 520.00
	Food	R 6 000.00
	Medical Aid	R 2 000.00
	Insurance	R 230.00
	Leisure	R 2 400.00
	Total Expenses	**R 20 350.00**
	Total Income	**R 20 000.00**
Step 4: Problem solve to generate more income	**Cash Flow**	**-R 350.00**

Table 2: Typical example of a budget

The presented budget table above might make it sound so simple, the fact of the matter is that it is simple, and a small amount of time and effort can have exceptional effects on one's financial future. The last point to understand about budgeting is that a budget is a plan and failure to plan is equivalent to planning to fail.

Now that we have established how to generate a savings pocket, let's examine how to use that money to make more money.

Chapter 4:

Knowledge is power

Seeing the rainbow and finding a pot of luck

University was a wonderful time for me, particularly the latter half, my grades were high, and the world was my oyster. I was afflicted with the illusion commonly experienced during one's youth, that of being bullet proof and unstoppable.

Side comment: Throughout my life I had managed to move from each step to the next with simple logical procession. Minimal thought or planning was required for me to reach the ultimate goal I had set out back in 2003, all that was needed was diligence and hard work.

However, then came the last few months of my studies, where I began my first real world lesson. One that I have carried with me every day since – Hard work, graduating engineering with distinction and having a resume filled with highly relevant vacation work experience was not enough for me to walk into a position at one of the country's top engineering firms.

"Hi Jordan, we would like to thank you for your interest in position ABC, however we regret to inform you that your application was unsuccessful." The preceding words is a short paraphrasing of many responses received from the hundreds of job applications I had sent out, amalgamating into only several interviews which lead to further disappointing rejections.

Naturally I began to become despondent.

The real world began to reveal itself.

Fortunately, my father, the aforementioned ever-determined man, helped motivate me to not give up and to persevere. At last, with less than one month to go before the final examinations I was given an offer of employment as a "Graduate Engineer" where I was to be part of a graduate programme for a large energy company. The stress had been lifted off my shoulders and my next steps where clear.

After having to go through so much effort to only land one job offer was an eye opener, it was clear that no one owed me anything, and even hard work didn't guarantee my success.

Side comment: Being honest, after receiving that position, I was elated and fell right back into the classical dogma of, get a high paying stable job and you will be rich and happy.

While realising that hard work doesn't guarantee success, I began to think of ways to ensure that I did not rely on others to help me succeed.

In hind sight, I count myself fortunate to have had the discipline instilled in me, during my childhood, to budget, pay myself first and then pay my expenses. As I have later come to realise that this is the only way to guarantee one's success. Soon after starting my first job I had saved and gained a small pool of capital (money to invest) and was keen to have that money make me more money.

Sitting at the country club overlooking the view of the ocean and green grass of the golf course, I found myself listening to a few of the local investors discussing, over a couple of cold beers, an investment they were involved in. The investors were discussing the merits of the fund that they were planning on investing in, hyping and encouraging each other up over the positive prospects of the portfolio of companies the fund planned to align with. Listening intently to the older, wiser more seasoned investors I couldn't help but share in their excitement, it was contagious.

But firstly, I wanted to conduct my own research. After searching the internet, reading a number of articles I was in agreement with the them, this was a great opportunity, one where we could take advantage of the power of economy of scale pooling our money together via the hedge fund. Now, by no means am I saying that the money that I had planned to invest had any comparison to the quantities the other investors were transferring in, however, therein lies the strength of a hedge fund.

Side comment: I can image reading this story may bring up questions or concerns such as, "I can't get into a country club and join a conversation about investing" or "Experienced investors won't talk to me, I haven't got anything to bring to the table". If those thoughts are coming up, I would like to make this point. Never underestimate the power of a kind smile, a keen interest and the humility to know you have a lot to learn, many people are welcoming to this demeaner.

Eleven months later, I sold my share of the hedge fund and bought myself my dream car cash. To this day I still have that car. While admittedly a car isn't a great investment, I cannot help but hold onto it. Not only because I love offroad vacations with my family and friends, but mostly because it reminds me of the fundamental life lesson that was imprinted in my brain the day I bought it – diligent saving combined with knowledge is a powerful way to achieve financial success, or in other words, not only is cash king when it comes to investing but information is as well.

When investing the hard-earned money that one has diligently being paying oneself, the number one aspect to consider is knowing where the money is going.

Four years later, this same lesson was driven home. This time I found myself on the opposite side of the story. I had rushed into investing in the same fund that had worked for me so well in the past believing that the fund managers were infallible and woke up one day with the fund having lost half its value and with it half of my hard-earned savings. I had forgotten the number one rule, know where your money is going.

Knowledge supremacies and information dynasties

I have often found that knowing where to gain knowledge and information about where and how to invest seems like a daunting task. When being faced with this seemingly impassible obstacle, I have noted that every time I simply get up and go out looking, knowledge or information falls in my lap. That sounds like simple advice however it's not exactly practical advice. So perhaps let me rather go through a few examples where I sought out knowledge and information and was lucky enough to find a pot of gold because I saw the rainbow.

Aside from the aforementioned instance where I gained information listening to knowledgeable people at the country club, there have been numerous other occasions where listening and discussing ideas in a social setting have helped me see the rainbow.

Sitting around a fire in the Drakensburg, surrounded by the shadow of mountains, and the sun having set behind them, I found myself in discussion with my dear friend Kevin, he had analysed a stock that he believed was under valued based on the impact the Covid-19 pandemic had had on it's public perspective, this business was focused on hotel lodging and while traveling had severely declined during the global pandemic, the business was set to regain strength based on the debt and asset restructuring it had strategically gone through.

Side comment: If the above financial jargon sounds complex and difficult to grasp, don't fret. At first understanding what my dear friend was explaining took me time to understand, however after a few pointed questions I saw the picture he was painting.

Once I got home, I decided to investigate the prospects of investing in the stock. I soon saw precisely what Kevin was talking about and decided to invest based on a 3-year investment plan.

The key take away here is not that one needs to understand everything about the financial and investing world but rather that one is willing to listen, learn and ultimately see the potential rainbow leading to a pot of gold.

In everyday life we are exposed to opportunities to gain financial knowledge or information, it is our keenness to see and understand that information that we are exposed to which will ultimately determine our success. It is pertinent to note that information does not have to only come from people but can also come from our surroundings and environment.

My friends and I had travelled to Ballito, South Africa, in that offroad car I had recently bought, two fishing kayaks strapped to the roof racks and keen to try our luck catching some Yellow Fin Tuna off the rocky coastline.

The next morning, after we had readied all the gear in preparation for our fishing adventure, we were standing, having a coffee, looking out the window of the apartment we had rented on Airbnb. The view of the turquoise ocean with the golden sun flecks skimming off the top of the waves was quite breath taking. I thought to myself, "I would have paid a lot more money for this experience, I can't believe the accommodation was so cheap."

Sitting out on the ocean the next day quietly paddling my kayak about in the hopes of hooking a massive tuna, I couldn't get the thought out of my head that the price of the accommodation was so cheap. "How could they be making any money?" I pondered.

I didn't bring back any Tuna that weekend. Though, reminiscing I have come to realise that I had in fact brought back something far better. I had learnt about an incredible financial opportunity. For the next two years, I diligently searched through property sales adverts seeking to "catch that Tuna".

Eventually I found a property for sale that was exactly what I had in mind, in fact, three were up for sale from the same owner, one required an extreme make over, another was in fairly good condition and the last, the one that I ended up buying, only required a face lift.

My wife Elyzka, who was my girlfriend at the time, joined me for the viewing. With her face painted with scepticism, she said, "I don't really see the value love, but I will support you." Quite frankly, I don't blame her for not seeing the vision I had in my mind, she hadn't experienced that epiphany I had two years prior, furthermore, at first glance, the flatlet did look like a dump. However, underneath that ugly exterior was true beauty ready to be exposed. It had the same breathtaking views I had looked out on, only this time it was hidden behind old glass windows which had become glazed over by years of sea breeze seeping between the double pane glass, besides the window it only required a deep clean and some minor handyman work to be presentable.

That property has been the investment I am most proud of thus far, it was the first of many investments into property and it inspired me to seek more opportunities like it. The best part of that investment was that it required none of my own money. I gained full financing for it which meant I didn't pay for the bond registration nor transfer fees with my own capital. Additionally, with the use of a credit card I let the bank invest a small amount on the face lift to turn it into a cash flow machine, making me richer.

Later we will go through the principles I followed which enabled me to use the money of others to transform another person's nightmare into my pot of gold. But first I would like to close this chapter off with what I hope to be a thought-provoking statement:

Knowledge can be found in the apple falling on Newtons head, it can be found in the motivation gained when reading a powerful book, it can even be the inspiration acquired when talking to a friend, the key to gaining it is the willingness to see, feel it or understand it.

So keep an open mind, be willing to listen, be willing to learn and ultimately, be willing to back yourself and take a chance.

Chapter 5:

Making money babies with passive income

Why passive income and not a retirement fund?

The topic of having sufficient money for retirement is something that is close to my heart. While sitting on my grandmother's porch, listening to her reminisce over days gone by, she paused and took a drag of her cigarette. Her face changed from a warm affectionate smile to a contemplative thoughtful expression, her wrinkles from years of laughter, slid into lines of worry.

Tapping the end of her cigarette off into the ash tray she said, "Jordy, I am a bit worried about my retirement fund, the young chap helping manage the portfolio is wonderful, kind, and puts on a brave face, however, I am no fool, I can see that the funds are running down and will eventually be depleted." Another puff of smoke later she continued, "I never want to be a burden on your mother and father and most certainly not to you or Daz."

I decided I would help my grandmother go through her accounts to see how we could ease her worries. The sad truth of the matter was that in fact her assessment was correct, her pension account was going to inevitably deplete one day.

That evening, driving home, I was caught in deep contemplation. How could it be that my grandmother, having lived by the rules, saving diligently each month, investing in her pension fund and other funds was now faced with this situation?

During her lifetime, global economic crashes (the Dotcom crash of 2000, the housing market crash of 2008, the covid-19 pandemic crash of 2020) had impacted her life savings to a point where her investments were significantly outperformed by inflation. What once would have been a fortune was now insufficient. Therein lies the fundamental difference between investing for capital gains or interest and investing for passive income.

Investing in financial assets that generate passive income have two critical advantages over assets that generate capital gains. Firstly, they are assets that are typically based off intrinsic value, property has an inherent value and often more than not maintains its value over the long term thus competing with inflation. Secondly, and I personally believe this is the most important aspect, passive income generating assets do not require a draw down on your principal capital during retirement. Thus, enabling a steady cash flow to pay for ones living expenses.

What does that even mean? Essentially, passive income assets provide money each month while holding their value, a property rental will yield rental income while not requiring any sale of the property itself, all the while maintaining its value relative to inflation. While capital gains income requires a withdrawal from the asset each month, this is usually taken from the interest earned attempting to not withdraw from the primary investment but rather from the interest earned over and above inflation. From my personal experience, I have witnessed family and friends find this an impossibility.

However, for arguments sake let's assume that money isn't taken from the investment and is only withdrawn from the interest earned, the fund is still required to outperform one's interest withdrawal as well as inflation. It is important that I point out that this is the general trend, there are cases where capital gains outperform passive income investments for instance in a bullish market. However, taking market fluctuations out of the equation, the principle of earning a steady flow of income while one's investment keeps up with inflation is fundamental to ensuring that one's financial freedom is sustainable.

To explain this concept even further I have included a graphical example where two charts show the effect of time and inflation on the two retirement investment paths. The example uses a one-million-rand property investment yielding a typical 1% of it's value in rental per month compared to a well performing one-million-rand investment fund producing a 10% annual return.

Figure 1 illustrates that the property value follows inflation, assumed to be around 5%, while the investment fund remains flat due to the interest/ returns earned being withdrawn monthly. Thus, the investment fund is reducing in actual buying power.

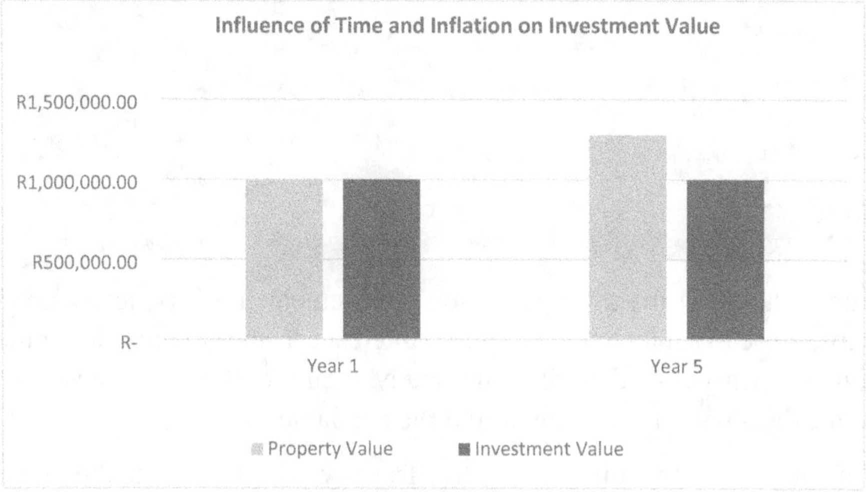

Figure 1: Graph of the effect of time and inflation on investment asset value

Figure 2 shows the impact on cash flow over time as the influence of inflation comes into effect. The rental cash flow follows inflation while the interest/returns earned from the investment fund remains flat. The investment fund cash flow thus falls behind ones living expenses which naturally increase with inflation.

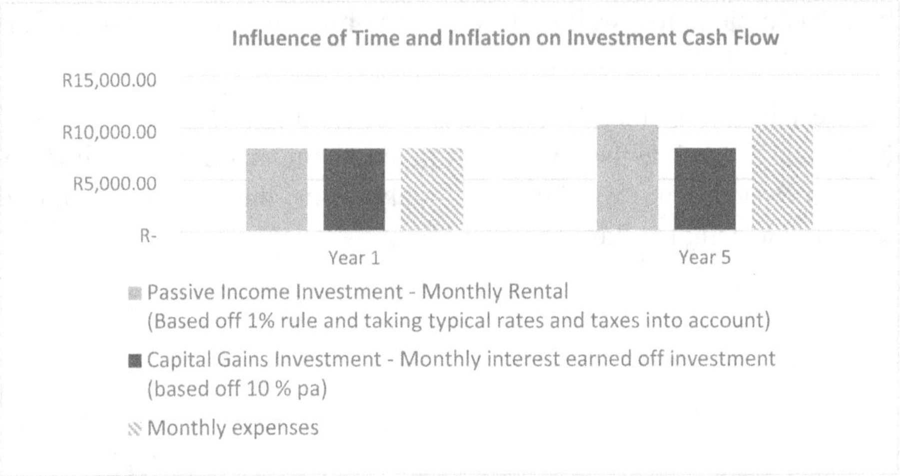

Figure 2: Graph of the effect of time and inflation on an investments cash flow

Funds that hold the average person's retirement funds typically do not come close to achieving the required interest earnings to provide for their living expenses and therefore, ultimately, their monthly withdrawals lead to the devaluation and depletion of the available funds.

One may argue that diligence to live frugally and only utilise the interest over and above inflation would make a capital gains investment just as good as that of a passive income investment. And yes, that is technically correct, if an individual had sufficient capital to sustain their living off the interest over and above inflation this method of retirement investing is perfectly adequate. However let us take into account another aspect that I believe is pertinent and cannot be ignored, that of human nature.

Considering how readily accessible one's retirement funds are later on in life, how likely is it that an individual will give into a temptation to purchase a luxury that would require them to dip into the capital portion of their retirement investment?

The phycological barrier due to additional effort being required to release capital from a passive income asset is a great way to prevent unnecessary spending, or at least make oneself think twice.

I would like to end off this point with a disclaimer, investing in passive income requires a significantly larger amount of initial effort when compared to investing in capital gains and the average person hasn't got the energy, at the end of their workday, to put towards anything else especially when one adds the energy requirements of family on top of that. The question one must ask is, "What do I want when I retire?". I personally found the answer to be quite simple and am willing to put in the hard graft while I am young to set myself up for when I am older.

Potential passive income opportunities

So now considering the compelling point that passive income can be superior to an investment into capital gains what possible passive incomes are there?

It was somewhat of a guilty pleasure relaxing and laying back on the cruise liners pool deck sailing around the Mediterranean while reading a book, all the while knowing that my honeymoon was paid for by passive income. Travelling through Europe, was truly spectacular, the food, people and experiences were completely different to what my wife and I were used to back in South Africa and what made it all the better was that it was paid for with money that had come in with almost no effort at all, better yet, money was still coming in even while we lay there enjoying the sunshine.

There is a great deal of possible passive income assets available in today's world. Some are easier to acquire than others and some have higher yields than others. The first half of Table 1, found in Chapter 1, illustrates some examples of the possible passive income assets available. Typically, there are three types of passive income generating assets:

- Property (Rental income)
- Business (Dividends income where control can be exercised over the asset)
- Shares or stocks on the stock market (Dividends income where control cannot be exercised over the asset)

Each type of passive income has its pros, and each has its cons, Table 1 touches on this topic however let's have a closer look.

Power of property

I have had many successes and many failures in my investment journey thus far and when it comes to property, I can honestly say that my investments have yielded some of my most successful steps towards financial freedom.

Investing in property has a great number of strengths that can be leveraged to generate a significant return on investment (ROI) and even in some cases an infinite return.

Side comment: an "infinite return" put in colloquial terms, is when an investment generates money for the investor off of other peoples money or put a little more formally it is an investment which generates a positive cash flow off of money loaned to the investor with the investor having put none of their own money into the investment, therefore the return on their capital invested is infinite as they never put any money in to begin with.

The idea of acquiring an infinite return investment seems impossible to achieve, surely if it were that simple everyone would do it. Well, I can personally attest to the fact that infinite return investments do exist, it just requires a bit of ingenuity and some imagination.

Returning to the first property I bought, the one I consider my best investment thus far, this property was and still is an infinite return investment. How was I able to turn the property into an infinite return investment?

Well, firstly, I had negotiated an exceptional price. Taking advantage of the fact that other investors were busy in a bidding war over the other two properties that the same seller had on the market. Their attention being focused elsewhere allowed me to swoop in and get a deal signed without any back and forth. This first point is the most important as when buying property money is made on the purchase price and not the sale price.

Second was that the timing of the investment was perfect, December vacation period was a few months away and my market research indicated that rental income during that period was unbelievably high. I say unbelievably because to this day I still cannot believe the prices people are willing to pay for accommodation over the December period in Ballito.

Once I had managed to get an agreement on the price I added a few caveats to the deal. I wanted access prior to the transfer going through for me to complete the minor maintenance work/renovations before the December holiday season. Additionally, I wanted my pick of the furniture that was being sold with the three properties.

Having received signed agreement, using my credit card to fund the renovation, I got to work sorting the property out, inviting some friends to help paint and remove old unwanted furniture, replacing it with the best furniture from the other two properties, we readied the place for the December beach goers.

Side Comment: Let's take a step back, how could I have put into the agreement that I was to have my pick of the furniture from the other units? The answer is quite simple, when it comes to a property sale the offer to purchase is a contract of sale, where almost anything and everything can be stipulated as a condition or clause. It's often amazing what a seller will agree to, to land a sale.

Once I had completed the minor renovations and furnished the unit all for "free" or in other words with other people's money. I put the property up for vacation letting. Mid-January came around and not only had I paid off the credit card bill for the minor maintenance, my first instalment on the properties loan and all the other running costs, I had also made a positive cash flow of R 6 000. By August I had generated sufficient profit to pay for a major renovation increasing the properties net value as well as helping generate even higher returns. Although, at the risk of sounding smug, I am not sure what is higher than infinite.

Reading this investment example may give the impression that investing in an infinite return property is simply a matter of following the correct principles and going for it. In a lot of ways that is true, taking the leap and going with your gut is a crucial part of the process, though, it is not wise to leap blindfolded. From the day of identifying the gap to earning that positive cash flow took close to two and a half years of market research, property viewings and negotiations.

Two and a half years sounds like a long time, and it is. Another two and a half years after acquiring my first property I found myself feeling despondent, sitting on my sofa in my lounge scrolling through numerous property listings, I could not identify another infinite return opportunity. While sitting their it occurred to me that while an infinite return opportunity is my goal, perhaps I was setting the bar to high, perhaps I would be able to make just as much money while also investing some of my own capital. With my new mindset it was one month, and I had identified a property, brokered a deal that was lucrative and would yield a positive cash flow, and taken the leap. Soon enough, or six months later to be precise, I had brokered a third deal leveraging the cash flow of the first property to gain financing for the next property and so this trend has continued.

In summary, there is power in property, and waiting for the perfect investment might take a lifetime. I have learnt to believe in jumping in and making the deal work, rather than falling into analysis paralysis.

With that said, it is wise to ensure that one has a plan and a back up plan for all investments. Such as if purchasing a property to renovate and flip is the plan, a back-up plan would be that the property is well located to become student accommodation.

That was precisely the case with a property investment my wife and I ventured into together. We purchased a property from desperate sellers mere weeks before it was going onto bank repo auction. The property was in a bad way with the previous owners not having had the funds to maintain it. We set out to renovate and turn the seemingly run-down property into a beautiful modern home.

When we purchased the property we had taken note that only a few blocks away was a new private university that had gone up, and thus our backup plan was to turn the property into a digs should the renovation plan not pan out.

Flexibility can be a great comfort when it comes to any investment, as in this dynamic world, being able to pivot can often be the difference between success and failure.

Let us move on to the next passive income generating machine, that of owning a business.

Being a boss, owning a business

Mark Zuckerberg, Elon Musk, Bill Gates, Jeff Bezos and Richard Branson all have one thing in common, besides having all had a million-dollar idea or being super-rich, these wealthy elite individuals run highly profitable businesses.

The average person has the perception that achieving the wealth of the super-rich is out of their reach, that being a billionaire, or even a millionaire is above them. Yes, achieving heights such as the aforementioned billionaires is difficult, however it is far from impossible.

The common investor would define a business as *an organisation or enterprising entity engaged in commercial, industrial, or professional activities*. Personally, I prefer to define a business as an entity which generates positive cash flow for the owner, because what's the point of owning a business if not for exactly that reason. I know that I personally don't want to own an asset with a negative cash flow.

When it comes to high yield passive income assets, business ownership can often be the highest performer. The difficulty lies with starting a successful business that yields a positive cash flow while requiring a low amount of time investment, ideally with a low initial cash capital investment as well.

How does ones go about doing this? The key to ensuring one's business has a positive cash flow in my opinion can be summarised into two core skills.

Firstly, and most importantly, sales skills. I know of several engineering friends of mine who have created, invented, or built an incredible product, something that could revolutionise the engineering industry, but have been unable to land any sales. Sales skills are not all that easy to learn, some often believe that people are only born with it. Fortunately, that is not the case, salesmanship is a skill that can be learned just like any other. Practice makes perfect.

The second critical skill to master is that of financial management. The skill of understanding cash flows, accounting, taxes, the list goes on. Ultimately, being an expert in financial management takes years of training, learning and practice.

Naturally, the question is then how can it be practical to acquire such a vast amount of skill in a reasonable timeframe? Practically and realistically speaking, it is unlikely that an individual could gain the skills required in their youthful years to be a one-man band business owner. With that in mind, the final thing that the famous people listed above have in common is that they surrounded themselves with people who had the skills that they lacked.

So that leads to the underlying essence of starting a successful business, don't try learning all the necessary skills required to start a successful business alone. If there was one skill to acquire to ensure the success of one's business, it would be the skill of being able to work with people or the skill of teamwork. In other words, being able to coordinate a team of people with the set of skills required.

Now that we have discussed the most important skills to have when starting a business, how does one protect themselves against failure. I believe it is common knowledge that most startup businesses fail. So how can bankruptcy be avoided when the failure happens.

Well, in chapter one, the benefits of leveraging ones guaranteed employment income was introduced, further to the financial leverage possible with that means of cash flow, is the possibility of utilising that income as risk mitigation against the failure of a start-up business. Now, starting a business can be a journey of learning on its own, filled with failures and successes, I use the word "failures" first as realistically a few failed business startup attempts precede a successful one.

Personally, I believe that it is best to begin the process of trying to start up a business with a backup plan, a.k.a. ones guaranteed employment income. This way one is not exposed to the turbulence of failure and success.

In short, the best way to start a successful business is simply just that, to start and to keep starting until one reaches success.

What about the stock market?

Many people would agree that the stock market is filled with risk, many more people would agree that knowing which share to buy on the stock market is seemingly near impossible.

First, before delving into the merits of the general persons sentiments towards the stock market, it must be pointed out that as an asset class, shares are not often the largest drivers of passive income but rather their benefit generally rests in their ability to provide capital gains. Now, that is not to imply that placing one's capital into the stock market is a poor decision as it won't yield high passive income, but rather it is to establish clarity and an understanding of the reason one would invest in the stock market as an asset class.

Ok, so we have established that the stock market is a great driver for capital gains more than it is a means of acquiring passive income, but the sentiment remains, how would one know which share to buy? Honestly there are a plethora of answers to that question. So rather than provide a synopsis of all the possible strategies to stock market investing I will simply provide my strategy that can be applied by anyone. When choosing which stocks to invest in, my strategy has been to stick to what I know. As an engineer, I have extensive exposure to the industrial sector as well as an in depth understanding of the workings of that field of business, thus when investigating which shares to purchase, I narrow the choices down to the businesses that align with my field of expertise.

During the early stages of my career, I began working in the pulp and paper industry. The insight I got into the world of paper manufacturing was invaluable to some of my first stock market investments. One day, while sitting in a maintenance planning meeting, a discussion came up about a business plan that one of our competitors in the industry were putting into motion. The business was proposing a large capital injection into their facilities and they were in the process of acquiring the funding. Later that day when I got home, I began to conduct some online research into the companies proposed business plan. I then looked at their latest share price performance and noted that based on the companies improved profit performance the share seemed to be undervalued. "Why is that?" I asked myself. After a bit of head scratching, I concluded that investors were reluctant to pay a higher share price due to the perceived risk of the upcoming business plan. Being in the industry and understanding the proposed plan as being something that was easily achievable, I realised that the perspective of the risk held by the stock market was misplaced and in-fact the share price was most definitely undervalued. Two years later I sold at a capital gain of just under 34%.

While a capital gain of 34% over two years isn't something to write home about, this personal anecdote of mine illustrates the strategy of de-risking an investment in the stock market by investing in what one knows. For example if I had exposure and expertise in the medical sector, I would focus my attention on medical or pharmaceutical companies or if I was in the retail sector my share portfolio would orientate around listed retailers.

This strategy has bode well for my financial journey thus far.

Another instance I recall was where I was sitting down at a braai area next to a lagoon, which flows past the little town of Mtunzini on the North Coast of South Africa, catching my breath after a paddle to the railway bridge and back, the conversations topic moved towards a potential investment opportunity, a mining company had received the rights to process rare earth metals from an old chemical plants waste product. At this stage I was working in the energy sector and was aware of the shortage of supply of rare earth metals used for the manufacture of permanent magnets that are fundamental to the green energy movement.

Armed with that knowledge I was extremely intrigued by the prospect of this investment. Again, using the power of the internet and my engineering background, I conducted a detailed investigation into the company's business strategy on how it planned to make a success of the rights it had gained to process the waste chemical stack. Looking through the high-level process plan that had been developed by the company to extract the rare earth metals, it became apparent that this company had a high likelihood of success. I moved as fast as possible to purchase shares before the market came to my same realisation. One month later, having transferred funds to the UK I bought shares of the company on the local stock market.

Four months after the purchase of the shares, their value had increased by just over 110%. Admittedly, the capital gains achieved on this investment exceeded my wildest expectations and provided me with a firsthand experience of the principal of market timing. I had realised that the market was behind the curve on the prospects of the company's success and profitability. I was also fortunate enough to have managed to act fast and acquire shares before the market caught up.

To summarise, when investing in the stock market, it is best invest in an industry that one has knowledge about.

Does investing still feel overwhelming?

If I were a betting man, I'd put my money on that answer being yes, it still does feel overwhelming. It's all good and well knowing what type of asset to purchase and being able to analyse and understand whether it is a great deal or not, but how does one even "buy" these financial assets? Is it the same as buying a car, or do you go to a special store where you swipe your debit card? Well, the next chapter will go into the detail and help try make sense of it all.

Chapter 6:

So how does one even acquire these passive income assets?

There are many ways to skin a cat

The actual process of purchasing any financial asset can be overwhelming, never mind passive income ones, and that's because today there are an incredible number of ways to go about it. Sometimes I think that the world of finance has been made overly complicated just to keep the general person confused, creating the need for financial advisors.

Side note: A prime complicated example is derivatives, this is essentially where derivatives of actual investments are manifested out of thin air, essentially creating money from nothing other than the notion of buying an asset, when in fact it is merely a newly packaged form of debt further removed from the actual tangible asset. Confused? So was I at first, so don't feel discouraged.

The modern financial system is complicated, and we won't get into why that is, but rather we will focus on simplifying the actual acquisition of an asset within it. Specifically, we will focus on how to buy the three passive income assets mentioned in the previous chapter, namely, Properties, Businesses & Stocks/Shares. Yes, I did say buying a business, because it is possible to purchase an already operational business.

So, let's delve into the details of each one.

Purchasing property's

By far, as I am sure has already been made abundantly clear, property is my favourite passive income asset class and like all the other financial asset classes there are several ways to purchase property. Some options provide direct ownership while some provide indirect ownership.

Side note: I use the term direct ownership to describe a state where one has direct control over the asset. (e.g. a property owned and registered to the investors natural person in their name). Indirect ownership refers to a state of ownership that has an intermediary and does not allow for direct control over the asset. (e.g. Purchase of shares in a property portfolio where the investor is seen similar to a shareholder on the stock exchange)

My preference is direct ownership of a property, as direct control over the asset provides an opportunity for me to personally drive improved returns. So, let's begin with how to purchase a property where one has direct ownership.

In 2022 I met one of the best property agents I have ever come across, she truly knew how to land a deal. I had been scrolling through a well known website www.property24.com , when I came across a deal that fit my investing criteria. At the bottom of the properties advert was the contact details for this star of an agent. A short phone call later, we had arranged a viewing for the next day so I could look at the property.

Side note: Always look at a property in person before putting in an offer. On most deals I would also advise employing the services of a professional property inspector.

After inspecting, I had a figure in my mind of what I was willing to pay, or should I say, what I would have the bank pay for me. In this case I began with a verbal offer to the agent who passed it on to the seller. The first offer was not accepted but a counteroffer was proposed, after a few text messages, a brief back and forth between myself, the agent and the seller a price was agreed. That same evening, a filled in offer to purchase document (OTP) with the verbally agreed pricing was emailed through to me for my signature and details. After reviewing the T's & C's, I sent it back that same night and the seller signed the next morning. Thereby concluding the agreement of sale.

The purchase process was not yet complete, however, I would like to pause here and go through the critical aspects of reaching this point. Firstly, the key to acquiring a property might be an estate agent but the key to getting a great deal is a great estate agent. The agent has the power to assist you as the purchaser to convince the seller to agree to your terms, they also have the power to cause the seller to demand for the asked for price be met. Having a top-notch agent is key to landing profitable deals. The second pertinent point to note, is that the agent guides the process of the purchase, enabling anyone to purchase a property, even if they are inexperienced.

Another important aspect to note which I left out is that it is pertinent to have in place, prior to the agreement of sale or OTP is signed, a comprehensive defects list detailing any issues that the seller is aware of with the property prior to sale. Fortunately, South African law has made this a legal requirement, although should one purchase a property in another country I would highly recommend insisting that one is put together and signed.

A known defect list can save the purchaser a great deal of pain and money at a later stage if something goes awry after the transfer process has been concluded.

I will illustrate this with a simple example I have personally been through. A property was sold to me stating that there were no issues with the servitudes and in particular the sewage systems. Later it turned out that the previous owner had actually covered a sewage line access point with a mound of garden refuge in order to mask the smell of the backing up sewage line. A brief phone call later, explaining to them the legal repercussions of what they had done, they had sent out a plumber to resolve the situation at no cost to me. Fortunately for all, it turned out to be a simple issue of roots blocking the pipe. That known defect list saved me a great deal of headache and from having to tackle a notably unpleasant job.

Ok, returning to the property deal we were discussing earlier, after the OTP was signed by all parties the next stage began, the daunting legal process. The truth is that the process isn't actually that daunting, it is just slow, as there are a large number of checks and balances that need to be completed before a bond is registered and a transfer goes through. This is to ensure that nobody is crooked.

With this deal I had included as part of my negotiation that both the bond registration attorney and the transfer attorney (a.k.a. conveyancer) would be from my preferred law firm. This provided me with both control over the time taken for the deal as well as a discount on the cost of the bond registration and the ownership transfer fees.

But wait, let's pause another moment, how did I even acquire a bond? Well at this point I had completed enough property deals and had developed a strong enough relationship with my bank that a bond approval process was more of a formality than anything else. But what if one has not got that banking relationship at their disposal just yet? Fret not, that star agent will come to the rescue, good estate agents often know, work with or have partnerships with a bond originator.

Side note: A bond originator is somebody who assists with finding the financing of a property deal through helping the purchaser during the bond application process. Something even better to note, is that these individuals are generally paid by the bank and don't require any of the purchaser's money.

Returning to the anecdote once again, after the attorneys drafted all the paperwork, contacted me to sign and had completed the leg work of getting the bond registered and property transferred, I was the new owner of another property, or more accurately, my property holding company was the new owner of another property.

Side note: We will discuss the basics of buying in one's personal capacity as a natural person or through some other form of or entity in a later chapter.

So, what are the important points to note from this recollection? Well, there is essentially one critical point to note and that is that the attorneys manage the daunting task making it a fairly simple process for the purchaser. Although, for it to feel simple it is always best to work with a quality law firm or attorney.

Does it still seems that there are a lot of steps, and appear complex?

I'll put it into a simple three step process.

<u>Step 1:</u> Find the property that fits one's required investment criteria and contact the agent.

<u>Step 2:</u> Let the agent assist with the deal negotiation, OTP and bond approval. The agent will then also likely assist with putting the purchaser in touch with the attorneys.

<u>Step 3:</u> Let the attorney's work on the legal process.

The three steps I am sure by now make it clear that the key to purchasing a property lies in the people who help along the way. They are professionals who will help manage the process and if they are good at what they do they will make it feel easy.

Now let's look at the possibility of purchasing property indirectly and what that process is exactly. This process is very much the same as buying shares on the stock market, or as being an "angel investor" for a company. To purchase property indirectly similar to the stock market one simply goes to a broker or trading platform. A quick google search will reveal a number of brokers or means of purchasing property like a shareholder.

Regarding the "angel investor" approach, this is simply where one loans their capital at an agreed upon interest rate to an individual, company or investor to assist them with the purchase or upgrade of a property.

Though as already mentioned, I prefer direct ownership without involving a middle person or entity, that way I can receive higher returns as well as enable infinite returns, earning money of other people's money.

Buying businesses

As discussed earlier, there is no doubt that owning a profitable business is a great way to become financially free. The difficulty is starting up a business that is profitable. A commonly heard line is "most business go bankrupt in their first 3 years." But what if there was a way of avoiding that initial startup phase and jump straight to stable profitable operation? Well, there are ways of doing that, namely buying into an already profitable business, becoming a partner or buying a business outright. Let's look at how one goes about actually doing that.

To start off let us discuss the "easiest" form being the outright purchase of a business. The process is much like the purchasing of a property but instead of brokering the deal through a property estate agent one brokers the deal through a business broker.

Using the various online platforms available, that a quick google search will help find, one can find and evaluate various businesses for sale, contact the respective business broker and begin the process of acquiring the asset. Personally, I wouldn't go about purchasing a business this way, instead my preference is to contact a business brokerage firm directly and describe the parameters that are required to be met in order for the deal to suit my criteria.

The challenge with purchasing a business in its entirety is that a profitable business is not often for sale. Something I am sure is obvious, but why would somebody sell a profitable business if at all? Well, there are very few reasons one would do that. While there are few reasons, there are in fact some reasons.

I will discuss one of the most common reasons one would sell their own business. It shouldn't come as a surprise that building a successful business requires a large amount of work, blood sweat and often tears. Thus, it should equally not come as a surprise that when someone is retiring from running their business, it would crush them to watch it fail just because they are no longer running things. In this situation, some opt to rather sell the business to a person they deem able to ensure that all their hard work building that business isn't wasted.

Aside from the rare cases of getting the opportunity to buy a successful business. there is then the more difficult form or manor in which to buy a business or more accurately, buy into a business. And that is the purchase of a portion of a business thereby becoming a partner. In my opinion this is the more difficult purchase as it is not only money that talks in this transaction, but also one's qualifications and value add as an individual. A simple example would be if one is an accountant, and the business seeks a strategic accounting partner. Similarly, to purchasing a business outright a business broker can be most helpful with putting one in touch with a business seeking funds and or a particular skill set.

Lastly, an alternative is the old school method of "keeping an ear to the ground" and listening for an opportunity or business to buy.

All things being equal, buying a business or a share there-of, typically requires a significant amount of time capital and often more than not, ends up not being an efficient passive income. Note, I say passive income, as often a business is a very effective way of generating large amounts of income, but typically not passively.

Stacking stocks

When it comes to passive income assets there is no asset that requires less effort than buying shares on the stock market. That's great, easy sounds good, but how does one actually buy shares on the stock market?

First let us begin with expanding on what the stock market is exactly. It was the year 1611 and the Dutch East India Company decided to raise funds to increase how much business they could carry out as well as derisk the business of trading internationally via ships, at that time, ships were at risk of falling ill to many forms of catastrophe such as weather, pirates, war etc.

And thus they developed an ingenious method of doing so – selling stock and sharing out the profits based on the returns of the stock purchased. This practice then developed further where in the late 1700's a small group of merchants created the Button Wood Tree Agreement, meeting daily to trade in stocks and bonds, this later transformed into the New York Stock Exchange. (Hwang, 2023)

For a long while, shares, stocks and bonds were traded in person in the form of legal agreements that were drawn up. These legal agreements were in effect loan agreements. The trading of these stocks then began being traded between parties excluding the original individuals/businesses with which the stocks were purchased from in the beginning, often in coffee shops. Meaning that coffee shops, as informal as they were, were the first stock exchanges. While it may sound rather uncontrolled and uncoordinated, there were in fact strict rules, for example in some exchanges a dress code was applied and one had to "gain a seat" to exchange in the market, there was also the matter of a membership fee. (Hwang, 2023)

Until 1971, the trading of stock remained a physical in-person paper exercise, that is until the National Association of Securities Dealers Automated Quotations (NASDAQ) enabled the purchase of shares via computers, thus allowing for the purchase of shares to be done by means other than physically being present. (Hwang, 2023) Moving the purchase of shares to an electronic platform opened the purchase up to the public at large however with the catch of requiring a person who has gained a seat to broker the deal for you.

The purchasing of shares may seem to have become a great deal more complicated since the earlier days, however, in fact, it hasn't changed all that much.

Today one can purchase shares or stocks with far less effort than before. The blessing of modern technology.

In my opinion, while it may have become simpler it has proportionally become riskier. Where before one would meet with a broker in person to affect the purchase of a companies shares or stocks, today one can simply go online and make a purchase, thus increasing the risk of fraud. So instead of discussing the many ways of purchasing shares in todays modern world let us discuss ways in purchasing shares while minimising the risks associated with handing over ones money to a possible fraudster.

To start off, the simplest way to purchase shares today is to download a share trading platform, an example would *Easy Equities*. Trading through a well know online platform or application has the benefit of making the process as simple as online banking and often equally as safe.

The catch with online trading via these platforms is that there are often clauses or catches which may introduce another form of risk to one's investment.

An example would be that often purchasing a "share" through these platforms is a trade where one enters a Contract for Differences (CFD), which, simply put, means that one enters into an agreement or "bet" on the shares with the broker. The advantage of a CFD is that the purchase is still seen as owning the share and is subject to many of same underlying principles of a share such as dividends payouts while not having to own a full share, the disadvantage is that one does not own the share directly which opens the investor up to a few risks that are often set behind the scenes. As with all investments it is highly advisable to go through the fine print, as tedious as that may be.

Another method of purchasing stocks in a risk adverse way, would be to personally meet with a stockbroker. An example of an institution which provides this facility would be *PSG* who are a professional investment managing company. Using the experience and expertise of a professional investment broker can be invaluable. But, their services aren't free, before investing through a broker one should understand their fees or in other words what percentage cut they will be taking.

Organising a meeting with a stockbroker is quite simple, all that needs to be done is to find their contact details online and make a phone call. Alternatively, one could even walk into the investment firms offices and request a meeting. These facilities are often more than willing to accommodate a walk in as their business is built on acquiring more assets under management thereby increasing the fees they are accumulating each month.

When it comes to investing ones hard earned money, as well as the not so hard-earned money that has come from one's passive income, it is critical to understand the fees behind the investments one would be making.

The saying that it takes money to make money almost always holds true. With that notion, let's look further into making money with other peoples money, specifically through property.

Chapter 7:

Buying that first property

Acquiring an infinite return

Earlier we discussed the first property purchase I made and which I view as the best investment I've made thus far. One of the reasons that I consider it to be one of my best investments is because it was made so early on in my investing career and at an infinite return. Managing to acquire an infinite return investment as my very first property purchase, I will admit, was something of an anomaly. The reality is that landing an infinite return investment on one's first deal is not common and is not usually an attainable goal. However, this does not mean that one should throw in the towel and give up before even starting.

Purchasing ones first property should be looked at through the eyes of somebody willing to pay their school fees, during that first deal I learnt so much simply by diving in. If I knew then what I know now I could have made the deal yield an even higher return, though I don't look at it thinking what I could have gained but rather what knowledge and experience I did gain.

In order to acquire an infinite return property there are a few key aspects to focus on. Let's go through them one at a time.

Firstly, there is one fundamental characteristic that should be looked out for when viewing various properties, and that is to see what others do not. See the potential that can be unlocked, see the beauty behind the mask of ugly, or put simply, be willing to put in the effort to make the property something worth more than what it was originally purchased for.

Following that, build a firm strategy around your idea, one that illustrates, to whomever you will be approaching for the capital, the potential of the property. The strategy can be in many forms and it is best to tailor your presentation to suit which ever entity you will be asking money from. Banks for example prefer a strong business plan, showing the potential returns, identifying what risks are involved, including plans for derisking the investment. Angel investors may like to see a slightly less formal plan and rather seek to understand the vision, albeit including sound financial numbers baking that vision.

Ultimately that leads to the primary crux of landing an infinite return investment. And that is the fact that one would be selling more than just the idea/vision/proposal to a potential investor but would also be selling oneself as a potential business partner.

There are seemingly an infinite number of places an investor could put their money. In order to gain access to their funds and achieve an infinite return for oneself the investment must be better than the other opportunities that lay before them.

Needless to say, achieving an infinite return is notoriously difficult in the beginning phase of ones journey, as almost all investors would not hand over their hard earner money to somebody who is “wet behind the ears”. Therefore to land an infinite return investment as one’s first property investment, the opportunity would have to speak for itself and one would need to show a great deal of determination that an investor would feel comfortable knowing that they would be handing their money to someone who will stop at nothing until the investment is a success.

Noting that the likelihood of convincing an investor to hand over funds to enable an infinite return investment for oneself is low for the first time property investor, how would one reach a point where they could actually achieve the experience level required to instil confidence in aforementioned those investors?

Well let’s look at that in a bit more detail in the following section.

Paying school fees

When talking to successful investors I have noted that they all have one thing in common, they are not afraid of paying their school fees. Constantly learning is the best method of reaching financial freedom and reading this book is a great step towards that end, but an even better step is to jump in and learn through practice. Practice makes perfect.

Significant money can still be made on the purchase of a property even if an infinite return isn't achieved on the first go. I personally believe that the best way to get started is to start small, pay one's school fees and get the ball rolling.

So, what does that practically entail, starting small?

In simple terms there are two ways of doing that, and the first is to literally start small, start with a small cheap flat, one that, should it prove extremely difficult to land a reliable tenant, the mortgage payments won't sink one's ship before it has even left the harbour.

The second way of reducing the risk is to put down a large down payment on the property. My suggestion, should one like to significantly reduce the risk of failure, would be to put down a deposit of more than 20% of the purchase price. Yes, this will drastically reduce the return on investment however, it is likely to reduce the school fees involved with making ones first deal as the property is far more likely to be cash flow positive from the get-go.

Pride is often what leads people to financial ruin, where people are to proud to accept a fairly mediocre deal as their first investment, people often want to view themselves as the Warren Buffets of the world and be the best at investing right off the bat, though they forget that Warren Buffet began investing when he was still in school and wasn't always the investment genius that he is today.

Starting off with a low risk, low return investment is wise and if anyone says different, I consider them as a gambler rather than an investor. I am not saying that one shouldn't ever take on the challenge of achieving an infinite return, but I am rather saying that it is wise to pay ones school fees before jumping in.

My school fees were paid through countless hours of research, which I am aware isn't everybody's cup of tea, so if reading and investigating every aspect of hundreds of deals isn't one's preference then the more practical manor of learning is through doing and making mistakes, and I would advise taking that approach with a risk averse style.

Aside from learning one's school fees, there are other strategies that would help protect against possible failure. One of those strategies is noting that one cannot know everything, and that having a strong team around you is invaluable. Let's discuss this point a bit further.

Developing a team

Investing in the property market can be likened to sport and like in sport winning requires having the best team and the best strategy. Being the investor is essentially the same as being the coach and captain of the team all in one, as the coach, one would pick the best players and as the captain one would guide the team to scoring.

What makes a good team? To answer that question, we need to investigate each position that makes up the team. In the previous chapter we looked at what are the steps to buying a property and touched on the people involved. The most crucial members required in one's property investing team are the estate agent, bond originator/ banker, conveyancing attorney and at times a construction manager. Each deal may not involve all the roles however having quality team members in each of these positions is crucial to ensuring a successful property investment career.

Let's start off with the Estate Agent and what makes a good one. There are many factors that could be listed as good characteristics a quality estate agent should have. For me the most important would be the ability to sell, not only to me but most importantly to the seller, an agent that can convince the seller to sign the deal makes them a priceless partner and asset in one's team. Practically testing an agent's sales ability, from my experience, can only come from time in the game. Working with and witnessing their negotiation skills comes with time and the more deals one works on, the more exposure one gets to different agents.

The next critical teammate is one who assists with the funding of one's deals. For example, I have worked on building a personal relationship with my bank to enable funds to be made readily available in the event of me identifying a lucrative deal. Again, this takes time. A faster route to acquiring funds reliably is by working with a bond originator, developing a working relationship with a person who has already made an inroad with individuals at the banks is a simpler way of ensuring that one doesn't miss a deal due to the lack of readily available funds.

Once the funds are available the ball is passed to the conveyancing attorney, there are attorneys that specialise in bond registration and ones that work specifically with property transfers. In my experience, the best quality to have in this specific teammate is that of timeous delivery. An attorney that is on top of the deal daily can make or break one's profit. It is always a long process having a bond registered and a property transferred though if an attorney is on top of the administration, the deal will go all that much faster. Additionally, if one would like to strategically slow down the transfer or registration for whatever reason, it is also helpful to have a quality attorney who can, through legal means, slow the process down. Note: It is a lot easier to slow down the process than to speed it up.

Once the property has transferred, or sometimes even before, it may be part of the strategy to begin renovating the property. This is where having a reliable construction manager/ contractor comes in. I can personally vouch for the fact that taking the cheap approach and hiring a "bakkie brigade" contractor is not the way to go. Identifying a reliable contractor is simple, they will always be on time, they do not look like a one-man band, and they will be semi-smartly dressed. If the contractor arrives in overalls and appears to have been doing all the work themselves then it is likely that they have been doing exactly that. In the construction world one gets what one pays for. If a high-quality job is required for the deal to be profitable, then a higher price would need to be paid, if the quality isn't too important than a less professional contractor is possibly a better choice.

Aside from establishing a strong working relationship with a reliable builder, I must caution one more thing regarding building projects that cannot emphasised enough. When contracting a job out, always, always establish the payment terms before the work begins.

I have had an experience where I made the mistake of not agreeing in writing what the payment terms would be. There were always a hundred reasons why the contractor needed more funds to get the job done, in hindsight, it turned out that he was using my funds to help fund another project he was working on. Do not make that same mistake.

The last member of the team, which I did not mention earlier as typically and in practice people only bring them onto the field at a later stage in their investing career, is a quality accountant. When I first started investing, I made the assumption that, based on my experience in business and ability in arithmetic, I could manage the accounting myself without the assistance of an accountant. Now that I know better I involve my accountant in almost every deal I make, understanding the tax implications as well as the profitability assessments.

Sitting at a sports club after finishing a hockey game I was jovially chatting with one of my teammates, who was an accountant and is my accountant today, the topic shifted to tax submissions where knowing he was an accountant I thought why not ask for some free advice. After a few questions he had established that it was likely that I could be significantly more efficient with my tax submissions and offered to manage my tax submission at “mates rates”.

Since I am never one to look a gift horse in the mouth, I readily agreed. That year’s tax submission was an eye opener, instead of paying the tax man, the tax man ended up paying me. I couldn’t believe it, I had been under the impression that I would be paying a sizable sum of tax due to the additional profits I had earned from my properties however with the correct allocations and cost accounting it turned out that, in fact, the tax man owed me money. Learn from my hardheaded foolishness and employ the expertise of a quality accountant, honestly, they will only save you money.

Now, on the topic of tax efficiency, there is another aspect that should be taken into account, something that I mentioned earlier in the book, and that is how to structure the ownership of one’s assets. To purchase in one’s personal name or to own the assets through a trust or company. This is a significantly complex topic and the following section will touch on some of the pertinent points to consider.

Trusting in trusts and opening close corporations

During my years at university, I was fortunate enough to build up a close group of friends from a wide range of professional backgrounds. One of my closest friends became a lawyer specialising in corporate law. Having a friend in this field has been invaluable, particularly in respect to receiving free legal advice in the area of corporate law, how and when to open a company and what structure to apply.

When it comes to tax efficiency, generally speaking, it is a great idea to utilise the reduced tax rates afforded to companies. However, should one purchase one's first property and register it in the name of a company rather than in one's personal name? The answer to that question would depend on one's personal circumstances, I will discuss the pros and cons of purchasing a property using a company rather than buying it in one's personal name.

As mentioned above, there can be significant tax benefits to purchasing a property this way, for example, in South Africa, company tax is 27% of the business's profits. For some people this is at a better rate than that of their income tax, Pay as you earn (PAYE). With that said, it is likely that when starting off on your investment journey one's salary will not fall close to an amount where one's tax bracket would be equivalent to or exceed 27%.

For me, this was the case when I first started investing and so it made sense not to purchase my first property in the name of a company but rather in my personal name as a natural person thus all the profits were taxed at my income tax rate rather than at the company tax rate. Over and above the savings on tax, I also saved on time and effort, as I only had one tax submission to worry about.

So, does that mean if one's salary falls within a bracket higher than the company tax rate it is best to purchase ones first property in the name of a company? Personally, I wouldn't believe that to be the best plan of action. Purchasing a property through a company has significantly more administrative processes and complexities involved, the accounting is without a doubt more onerous, and the legal aspect of transfer is more difficult. Realistically, when purchasing one's first property, the likelihood of having established a strong team prior to purchase is low. I would advise purchasing one's first property through a company only if there are significant tax benefits to be gained because of one's personal income tax bracket.

With that being said, the best advice I could offer would be to take the time to sit down with a professional such as my friend from university, who specialised in corporate law, and go through the best course of action.

With us having established some of the core principles involved in taking one's first steps in investing in property, let's look at some of finer details. Such as what type of property to buy, where to buy it and when.

Chapter 8

What, where & when

Picking a property type

The world of property is vast and can seem overwhelming due to the number of options to choose from. In a broad sense, property can be divided into four categories, namely industrial, commercial, agricultural and residential. To choose which category best suits ones portfolio it is best to understand a few of the defining factors and attributes of each one.

Industrial property typically has the following characteristics:

- Large capital outlay (ie. industrial property generally isn't cheap)
- High tax rates for the land and buildings
- High rental rates (In the right deal high yields can be achieved)
- Typically owned by a business and VAT would need to be taken into account when purchasing the property.

In short, industrial property is a high cost, high potential yield investment, with the high costs there are significant risks involved. For example, should a tenant default or the property remain vacant for a significant amount of time then naturally the property can become a massive liability.

In 2023, while sitting in a sunroom, overlooking the two dams of our family friend's trout farm close to Nottingham Road, I was enthralled in a conversation regarding various property investments, discussing ventures that my family friends had embarked on and what were the results that they had achieved. When we began discussing their industrial property investments, they admitted that out of the many property investments that they had worked on throughout their lives they had found that their industrial property assets had performed the worst. Vacancies and high costs with low capital gains had yielded a poor return on their initial capital.

In my opinion, as a property type, industrial property is an investment type which should only be entered into once one has gained a large amount of experience.

Commercial property can be split into two categories, firstly office space letting or rental and secondly retail letting or rental. The first has very similar characteristics to that of industrial property. The only difference being that in recent times, the need for office space has reduced significantly as more businesses are allowing "work from home". Thus, the demand for office space has decreased to a point where, while writing this, the market has flooded with office space properties. If one is innovative, one could find great deals in this property type and pivot it into a more modern form of office letting where offices and boardrooms are let for the day to individuals rather than entire businesses. Again, like with industrial property, in my opinion this property type requires extensive experience prior to investing as the costs are significant and can lead to severe financial stress if not properly prepared. The deals I have investigated in this market have held too high a risk requiring me to front large amounts of my own capital in the case of things going wrong and thus I have chosen not to invest in this market space yet. Perhaps one day I will find a deal in the commercial space which fits my investment criteria.

Moving on to *Agricultural Land* and its characteristics. As a property type, agricultural land isn't typically a passive income generating asset class. Farming is hard work and requires a great deal of time so aside from those individuals who want to retire to the countryside and work the land, I wouldn't advise using this property type as an investment tool, unless one plans to rezone the land into another type thus opening the possibilities up significantly. At the time of writing this, rezoning agricultural land is what I am currently working on. I am investigating rezoning a piece of agricultural land to Industrial Zone 1 allowing storage rental facilities to be built. Again however, caution is required when adopting this property strategy as the rezoning of land is wrought with administrative and legal hurdles which can often be crippling stumbling blocks.

The last property type is *Residential property,* in my opinion, residential is by far the best property type to start off with. The capital and costs involved are typically not exorbitant and are affordable to the general person. An added benefit of residential property is that it is easier to find a motivated seller who is willing to sell at a reduced price thus making it more likely that one will be able to achieve a higher yield. Residential property is characterized by:

- Lower capital outlay
- Lower tax rates
- Medium rental rates (Fair yields can be achieved)

There are many types of residential property types that one can invest in however the simplest to start off with is a "flat".

Aside from the potential yields and risks involved with each type of property, one also needs to consider capital gain trends. Figure 3 below illustrates the transition of capital as we have moved into the twenty first century. Capital in the form of housing has grown steadily while capital in the form of agricultural land has reduced drastically. The driving force of this trend is fairly obvious, being urbanisation and the worlds population boom. In the long term the trend may taper off, however, in my opinion, that is unlikely to be the case over the next twenty to thirty years. Note, the trend in Figure 3 may be based off data from the United States, however the same trend can be seen across most of the world. Now, focusing on and specifically looking at South Africa, a very similar trend is likely to be seen, as the working class grows so will the demand for entry-level middle-class housing.

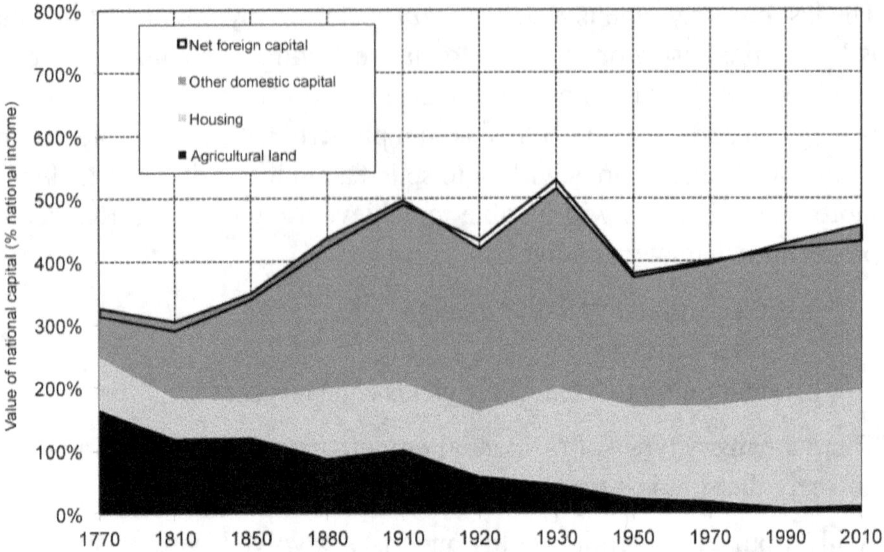

Figure 3 Capital in the United States 1770 to 2010 (Piketty, 2017)

It is important to note that Figure 3 is a macro level view, when one is looking into a property to invest in, one should also take into account the micro level trends, which leads to the next section of this chapter, where to purchase a property.

Location, location, location

Most people have heard the phrase "Location, location, location". But what does it actually mean? And how does one even know where is the right location?

Establishing where to purchase a property is easier than it may seem. There are a few principles that I have learnt during my investment career that when applied can help ensure that one buys in the right place. These principles are basically driven by one fundamental aspect of any good financial deal, supply and demand. Understanding the supply and demand of a property in a given area will quickly help establish whether or not it is a prime location to buy. At times, it does take vision to see what others don't, however for the most part following the trend can also be highly lucrative.

Let's begin with understanding what drives the supply of a property type and what are the ways to see whether the supply is in surplus or in deficit.

Firstly, supply is driven by investors being willing to invest their time and capital into an area, typically this can be seen by driving or walking around an area looking out for building projects underway. The more building projects that are being undertaken in an area, the more people are willing to invest in that area and drive the supply of property. A risk to take note of here is that often large investors and developers identify an opportunity and flood the market thus pushing the supply into a surplus.

The way I identify a surplus of supply is by going onto the internet and looking through properties that are available for rent, I look at how long they have been advertised for, how many have reduced their asking price and how many newly listed properties are on the market compared to how many are being taken off. If the trend shows that properties are stagnant and not being rented out, I will consider the area to be experiencing an oversupply or a reduced demand.

Earlier in the chapter we touched on the demand side, but what actually drives the demand of property. While there are many contributors to property demand, the overarching factors are those that have stood the test of time and an intrinsic need of all humankind. The need for shelter can be used to some it into a single point. So, in order to understand what drives the demand for property, one needs to understand what drives the need for shelter. Based on my perspective, people have an intrinsic need for shelter due to the following reasons.

Firstly, people need a place to sleep, a place to lay one's head and rest is something that is required ultimately for survival and is a need that isn't likely to disappear anytime soon. The second aspect leads off from the first and that is the need for safety, as I am sure is obvious, when sleeping one would need to feel safe. The third point, and the last one I will mention, is that people have a need for comfort. While this isn't a basic need it is a high priority in peoples lives that I believe exceeds the level of only being a want.

When people work long hours and need rest, it is built into them to want a place where they can rest not only safely, but also in comfort.

Thus, when trying to understand whether there is demand for property in a location, ask the simple question, "Does the property provide shelter in all its forms?"

To illustrate the point a bit further I will provide an example, a high demand property would be one that is:

- In a gated community, thus providing safety.
- In a safe area with low crime rates, further adding to safety.
- Well designed and aesthetically pleasing bringing a feeling of comfort.
- Close to crucial amenities, thus affording the comfort of short travel times and convenience.

Now that the basics drivers and points of supply and demand have been covered let's move onto the next topic – when to buy and at what price.

After deciding on the type of property one would like to buy as well as where to buy it, one would begin looking into what price is right for that deal.

Buying at the bottom, selling at the top

Understanding what a reasonable price to pay for a property is can be a difficult and often confusing task. Property prices are based off people's opinion after all. Or are they?

There are many factors that determine the price of property. However, throughout the age of man there has been one core driving principal that has determined the relative magnitude of a properties worth, and that principal is what is known as the One Percent Rule. The One Percent Rule in words is where a properties rental should bring in approximately one percent of its overall worth per month.

Often people apply the One Percent Rule to determine what rent is reasonable to charge a tenant, however that is in fact the rule being applied in reverse. In a world where cash flow is king, and the real determining factor of worth is how much revenue an asset can generate, it only makes sense then that the One Percent Rule be applicable to determine a property's value rather than the other way round.

So am I saying that, when buying a property, simply pay a price according to the One Percent Rule? Well, no not quite. When I investigate an area to purchase a property I apply the One Percent Rule as a guide to identify possible lucrative deals, I then seek out deals which are better than the typical 1%. In reality I try find deals closer to 2%. Applying this approach enables what I like to think of as breathing space in case I need to reduce the asking rental price if the market has slowed or if I made a mistake during the investment analysis.

Example: Looking through one of the many property advertising platforms I come across a property which is listed for R 1 Million. After looking through the areas rental prices, using often the same property advertising platforms, I note that the rental income from properties of the same type average around R 12 Thousand Rand per month. Immediately I note that there is a gap in the market where this property has already beaten the 1% rule based on the listed price. From there, should I like the property, and the analysis indicates that a positive cash flow may be generated, I would then engage the agent and use my negotiation skills to land the deal as close to the 2% mark as possible.

Ok, now that we have established an understanding of the One Percent Rule and its application, what are the driving forces of rental prices and overall property price? This is another occasion when the answer may at first seem quite complex though the overall idea is actually quite simple. Property is much the same as any other goods, service or commodity and its price is also driven by supply and demand. This is where the complexity comes in. Let's build on the previous section and look further into what drives supply and demand? To simplify the answer further lets look at the following scenario:

John and his wife, Mary, are newly weds looking to purchase their first home. After assessing their finances they realise that their affordability is not going to enable them to purchase the dream home that they had envisioned. John has not received an increase in two years due to the tough economic climate and Mary was recently retrenched but managed to find another job, albeit at a lower salary.

Even so, they are determined and won't give up on their dream and are driven to find a home that fits their criteria.

Now let's look at Fred, a father of two boys. He comes home to his wife Sarah one day with a worried look on his face, he has lost his job. Being the bread winner for the family, they are now under severe financial strain. While their savings may last a few months, at some point if Fred doesn't find work they will need to sell their home. A few months go by and Fred realises with dismay that the economy is weak and work is scarce. He and his wife make the hard decision to sell their home.

Returning to Mary and John, who have been relentlessly searching for the right property, see the advertisement for Fred and Sarahs home online, the price is outside their affordability range however they decide to go view it anyway. After their viewing they cannot help but fall in love with the property. As soon as they get home they begin looking into ways in which they can afford it. Unfortunately, realise that they will never make the full asking price.

Not giving up hope they decide that they will put their best offer on the table and see if the seller, Sarah and Fred, will accept it.

When Sarah and Fred received the offer to purchase from John and Mary they were disheartened, though relieved. They had not received an offer in months and while the offer was significantly less than what they had bought the house for initially; it would at least cover the remaining bond and selling costs. Added to that the bank had begun to plan to repossess the property, and they were just glad to be able to avoid that terrible outcome.

Mary and John receive a call the next day from the estate agent and to their astonishment, Fred and Sarah have signed and accept the deal.

The scenario above provides an example of one of the many the drivers of supply and demand. The important point to take away from this is that to find the best deal, is to find the most motivated seller.

This fact is even more pertinent to take note of during tough economic times where the number of people buying property drops significantly due to a multitude of factors such as banks providing less loans, lower employment rates, increasing interest rates etc.

During tough economic times one can often find great deals, however this does not mean that during strong economic times great deals don't exist. The important aspect to grasp when gauging the right price for a deal is whether it is a buyers or sellers' market, and these do not always align precisely with the current state of economic affairs.

Economists love to delve into complex numerical and statistical analyses of markets. Where they try to understand and forecast predictions about what is and what is going to happen. I believe however, one can simply gauge people's general sentiment to understand whether it is a Buyers or a Seller's market.

Perhaps we should pause for a minute, what is all this about Buyers and Sellers markets? And which is which?

Simply put, a buyers' market is where the buyer holds the power during the negotiation, Mary and John for example found themselves in a buyers' market where there was ample supply of properties with people faulting on bonds and very low demand with very few people being able to purchase a property.

A sellers' market, on the other hand, is when the general economy enables a significant number people to enter the market driving up demand or it could be that the number of people selling reduces due to stable economic times or even where there is sentiment that property prices are on the rise leading to people holding out from selling hoping to get a higher capital return in future.

It may be tempting to think that it sounds simple and timing the market is all that is required to succeed in property investment. However, regardless of which market is at play, caution should be taken when delving too deep into or focusing too hard on which type of market is afoot.

I have purchased property during both market times, buyers and sellers, and have come out on top either way. And this brings me to the overarching point regarding what price to pay for a property. Landing a great deal simply requires an understanding of which market is in affect and to work on property deals accordingly.

I am sure it is now tempting to think that a detailed understanding of economics is required, particularly Macroeconomics. However, this is not completely necessary, while it is helpful.

Understanably with all the moving parts, gaining an understanding of Macroeconomics is a lengthy and difficult affair. Thus, in order to simplify the process, the following chapter will cover some of the facets of Macroeconomics that I have found to be more pertinent to my own personal finance.

We will leave the in-depth study of global political drivers and some of the other factors that affect the global and local economy for another day and instead focus on the core concepts of a countries fiscal policy, including the effects of inflation and interest rates on one's personal financial situation.

Chapter 9

Thinking Macro

Why think about the macro?

At this point the natural question being asked is why even think about the macro and global economic ongoings, especially since as an individual one has no control over the day to day changes of the bigger picture. To answer that question lets consider the following example from my personal experience.

The global financial pains of Covid-19 had piled up, interest rates were high, inflation was climbing globally and people were struggling to put food on the table never mind pay mortgages or rent. The economy was in what is known as an economic slowdown.

Noting that, from a macro point of view, people were struggling, I identified an opportunity, with people being unable to pay their mortgages, the default rate was high and properties were being sold at a discounted price either by bank repo auctions or by sellers desperate not to get black listed.

I began searching for a bargain, identifying an area which was affluent and then finding a seller who was extremely motivated to sell. My understanding of the macro-economic situation being faced by the world enabled me to identify a gap in the market that had opened up, then after investigating thoroughly in that gap I found and bought a property at an absolute bargain. In fact, I purchased the property at a price 15% lower than what the seller still owed on the bond.

Note: One may think that it is immoral to purchase a property at such a low price leaving the seller still owning a portion of the bond. However, when you take note that the sellers property was about to be placed on auction two weeks later where they would have ended up with less money after all the auction expenses, the purchase price offered was then actually a win win for the seller and myself. They reduced the debt owed to the bank after the transactions completion and I received a discounted price on the property.

Additional note: This deal ended up being at such a discount that SARS flagged it for an audit to ensure that everything was above board and that the correct transfer tax was being paid. This is common for commercial properties however not very common for residential properties.

Once the gap has been identified and a possible great deal has been found, it doesn't help to buy a property at a discount when the property prices will only continue to decrease, and this again is where the understanding of macroeconomics comes into play. I had noted that on a local level, South Africa was set for an economic turn around and that on the global level the world was showing signs of preparing to do the same. One year later after buying the property the economy had strengthened significantly, and the property value had increased 35%. Albeit with a significant amount of elbow grease put in by my wife and I.

Undoubtedly it is extremely sad what happened to the sellers that I bought this property from, however, as mentioned, through the purchasing of the property I had helped the seller avoid being blacklisted and thus saved them from complete destitution and in actual fact, 9 months later they had gotten back on their feet and I bumped into them walking their dogs through the suburbs after they had moved back to the area.

Taking a step back and looking at the above example pragmatically it is clear how having a fundamental understanding of the Macroeconomics around one's environment can help reveal amazing opportunities as well as reveal risks one should take into account.

Alright, now that we have covered the why, lets discuss the how. How exactly, did I know that the economy was set for a turn around? Well let's take a look at some of the key indicators.

Indicators of the global and local economy

The truth is that understanding economics isn't as complicated as economists would have you believe. As Nassim Nicholas Taleb puts it in his book *Skin in the Game*, the extreme complication of some facets of life is simply due to some people justifying their roles through adding complexity where there need not be.

Before I get too philosophical, let's jump right in. In general, the local and global economy follows a wave like pattern with periods of growth/expansion and periods of decline/contraction.

Hang on, that sounds complicated. But if one reads that sentence a bit slower it isn't really all that complicated, put another way, there are good times and there are bad times and those times occur cyclically. The figure below shows a basic illustration of this phenomenon.

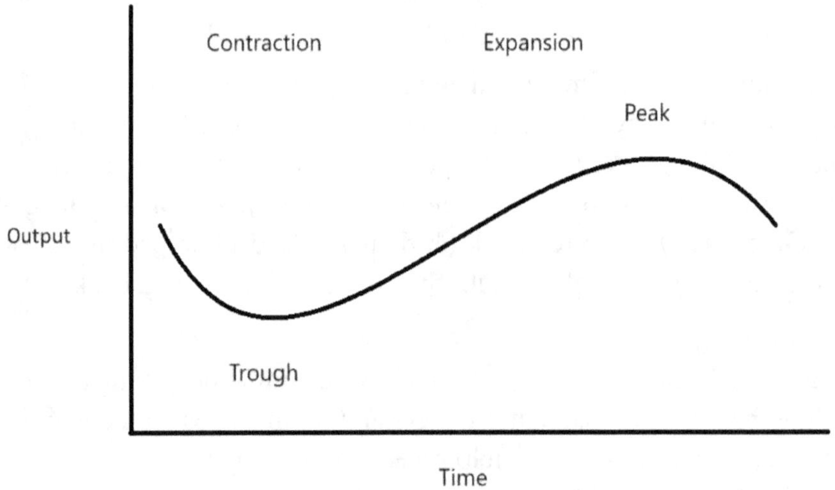

Figure 4 General illustration of the economic cycle

There are numerous drivers that cause the economy to behave in this way but from my experience it is more important to know where one is in the cycle than to understand why it occurs. So, lets focus our attention on understanding our position in time rather than why we have ended up there.

To understand at what point in the cycle we find ourselves in, one needs only ask a simple question. Are people optimistic or pessimistic? And then one must try gauge what level of optimism and pessimism the general public has. The psychology of humans is a fascinating subject, one that can be discussed at length, however one key aspect of the human psyche that I have noted and found most helpful when gauging where in the economic cycle we stand, is that people tend to be "short sited" for a lack of a better term.

During times of economic growth people naturally become optimistic, and as in the economic cycle that optimism reaches a peak. Similarly, during times of economic hardship people tend to be pessimistic and also reach a trough in levels of pessimism.

Thus, noting the similar cyclical pattern of the general public view, ie optimistic or pessimistic, it is fairly straight forward to correlate it to the actual economic position. The figure below illustrates the correlation.

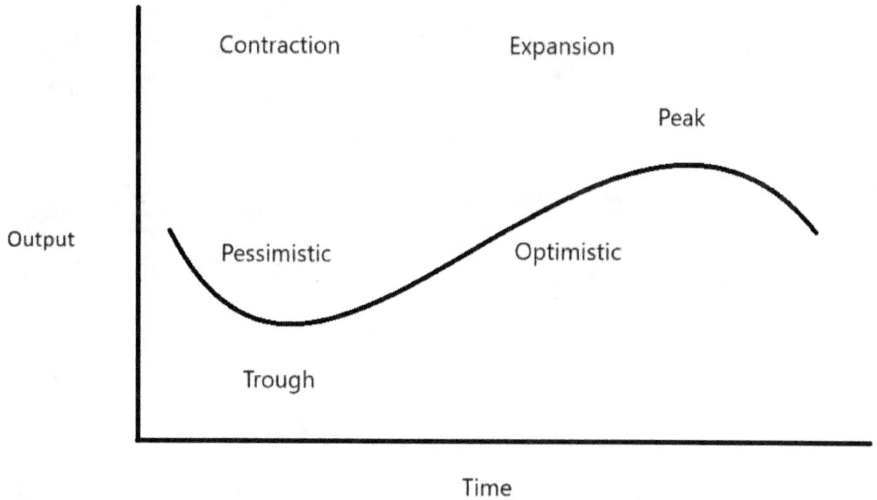

Figure 5 General illustration of the human economic psyche cycle

The most important points in time when it comes to economics, in my opinion, are those where we find ourselves in a trough or peak. The best opportunities can be found during times of extreme pessimism where the economy is at its lowest with jobs being scarce, people struggling to make ends meet and a general presence of dread is in the air. Furthermore, when there is extreme optimism and people are talking as if we are all invincible, this is a time to prepare for the downturn.

While understanding the overarching flow of the economy through time is one of the most crucial skills to learn, gaining an understanding of some economic specifics will also be useful.

Next, we will discuss some of those specifics that I believe are most pertinent.

Some specifics

Inflation, what is it and why is it? My definition of inflation simply put is the increase in cost of goods, assets and services through time. Note, I say increase as this is the general trend, however there are times where deflation can occur which is the general decrease in cost of goods, assets and services through time.

For now, let us focus on inflation. The driving force behind inflation is complex and many theses have been written about its drivers and causes. I'll rather focus on its effects. As the cost-of-living increases so does the value of one's assets. So, what role does this play in personal finance? In short it is best to be on the side of owning assets than on the side of the consumer. Thus work on positioning one's portfolio as being asset heavy and liability lite is fundamental to driving future capital gains and wealth creation.

Note: I specifically state that the value of one's ***assets*** *increases when coupled with inflation, this is to emphasise the importance of purchasing assets and not liabilities. Things like cars and various other "goods", aka liabilities do not typically increase in value with inflation and remembering that will help provide that extra bit of motivation to avoid superfluous purchases.*

Aside from how to position one's financial portfolio the next important point to understand, is how inflation impacts the general public. During times of high inflation people begin to struggle to cope with the cost of living as the cost of consuming goods out strips the growth in their salaries. This begins to lead to times of pessimism. Couple this with the next aspect that follows high inflation, which is high interest rates and you'll begin to find motivated sellers all over.

This brings me to the third specific point I would like to touch on and that is the method countries try use to control inflation. Countries try control inflation through their central banks who increase interest rates during times of high inflation. This in turn reduces spending by making loans more expensive and further increasing financial strain on the general public. Reduced spending leads to lower demand and thus pressure on prices are created where suppliers reduce prices in order to try retain market share.

The fourth and final specific point I would like to touch on is one that is somewhat ironic. During times of financial optimism, where people feel that they are managing their finances well and are increasing their wealth, they tend to stretch their finances to the maximum extent they can taking on large amounts of debt while inflation/interest rates are low. Then comes the ironic part, the market changes, these people who believed they were doing great financially find themselves in the time of dread where faulting on loans begins.

And, if one has managed one's finances properly, avoided bad debt during the optimistic financial times and has spare cash or cash flow, this is where opportunity lies.

Chapter 10

Tying it all together

The field of personal finance is often seen as daunting and I hope that the content covered here has helped provide a useful guide to the intimidating task of navigating ones finance and ultimately achieving financial freedom. I have always found that a recap of core concepts helps them set in. So let us go through a short summary of what has been covered. The below diagram can be used a quick reference guide.

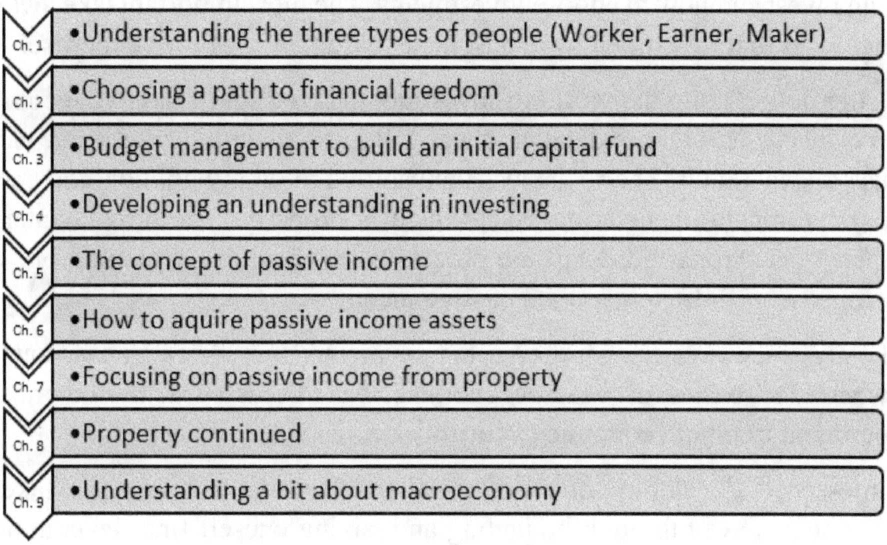

Figure 6 Short reference diagram of topics

Initially we started off with gaining an understanding of the various ways in which one can generate an income. The concept of the three types of people was covered and the idea of a Maker was established. As I am sure is clear after reading this book, being a Maker is my preferred position. We also went through the concept of financial freedom here. With this understanding we then moved onto to looking into the various ways in which one can gain financial freedom.

The method of achieving financial freedom I most believe in, is that of choosing the best of both worlds. Here, we discussed how to leverage ones stable income from standard employment in order to drive the increase of passive income through earning money off other peoples money. From there we moved onto the concept of budgeting, often the most difficult aspect of becoming financially free. The core take away here is that one should pay oneself first then pay others. Through budgeting and paying oneself first an initial capital amount can be built up.

The next topic then went through some fundamentals regarding ways one can invest and how to choose investments. The most important take away here was that investments are best made based on ones own expertise.

After delving into the world of investing, the concept of passive income was discussed in more detail and was followed up with methods one can use to generate it. The focus was then shifted to, in my opinion, the best passive income generating asset which is property. The next chapters then went through in detail the processes involved in developing one's property portfolio to generate passive income.

Lastly to end off the journey a bigger picture was taken into account where the basics of Macroeconomics was discussed with the most pertinent trend of economic cyclicality being the key focus.

In essence, developing one's financial freedom and becoming a Maker can be achieved through budgeting and paying oneself first, leveraging ones stable income, investing in what one knows as well as passive income generating assets and lastly taking advantage of economic cycles.

When in doubt, I always believe in keeping it simple. And in the end nothing can replace hard work, but ensuring that one's hard work is guided in the right direction can lead to the biggest rewards.

I wish you all of the success in your journey to financial freedom and I hope this book has equipped you with the tools necessary to experience life fully.

Afterword

Throughout this book we have put a great deal of focus on money, however I would like to add that happiness in life is not measured by how much money one has. True wealth isn't defined by the size of one's bank account but rather the quality of one's life.

In my opinion, the idea of true wealth is best defined by the American Philosopher, Henry David Thoreau "Wealth is the ability to fully experience life." While I have spent the last 100 or so pages going through ways to make and accumulate money, it is critically important to know this truth.

So before embarking on a journey to wealth or before continuing, I would highly advise that one sits back and assesses what would truly define the point at which success has been reached.

If you ask my wife she'll tell you about how I always go on at length about how any goal has to be a SMART goal (Specific, Measurable, Achievable, Realistic, Timed). I believe that in the case knowing what one's definition of finally reaching financial freedom SMART goals both apply and don't apply and, at the risk of being told by my wife that she was right and that not all goals have to be SMART ones, when it comes to financial freedom it is important to acknowledge that true financial freedom is measured by the feeling of being free, so in a way, it is difficult to apply a SMART goal to a feeling.

I would instead suggest identifying the things that would truly give a sense of freedom and use that as a measure of whether or not financial freedom has been reached. For example, not having to work in order to make the payment of the monthly bills or perhaps it could be having sufficient money to afford an annual vacation.

To end I would like to make this final point, knowing what defines one's financial freedom will help with more than just being able to know that one has reached it, but it will also help one actually enjoy it when one finally does.

References

1. Hwang, I. (2023, June 15). A Brief History of the Stock Market. Retrieved September 14, 2023, from SoFi: https://www.sofi.com/learn/content/history-of-the-stock-market/
2. Laskow, S. (2014). How Retirement Was Invented.
3. Piketty, T. (2017). *Capital in the Twenty-First Century.* Cambridge , Massachusetts, London, England: First Harvard University Press.
4. Robert L. Clark, L. A. (2003). A History of Public Sector Pensions in the United States.
5. Weisman, M.-L. (1999). The History of Retirement, From Early Man to A.A.R.P. *The New York TImes.*

Notes

1. Benjamin Graham, *The Intelligent Investor* (New York, HarperCollins Publishers, 2003)
2. Thomas Piketty, *Capital in the Twenty-First Century* (Cambridge , Massachusetts, London, England: First Harvard University Press, 2017)
3. Robert Kiyosaki, *Rich Dad Poor Dad* (Scottsdale, First Platta Publishing, 2017)
4. Jason Lee, *Making Money Out of Property In South Africa* (Cape Town, Penguin Random House, 2019)
5. Laurens Boel, *Financial Freedom Through Property* (Cape Town, Penguin Random House, 2020)
6. Laurens Boel, *Millionaire In the Making* (Cape Town, Penguin Random House, 2021)
7. Peter Thiel, *Zero To One* (Cape Town, Penguin Random House, 2014)
8. Warren Ingram, *How To Make Your First Million* (Cape Town, Penguin Random House, 2016)